300
handcrafted
SOAPS

300 handcrafted SOAPS

Great Melt & Pour Projects

Marie Browning

Sterling Publishing Co., Inc.

New York

Prolific Impressions Production Staff:

Editor in Chief: Mickey Baskett
Copy Editor: Phyllis Mueller
Graphics: Dianne Miller, Karen Turpin
Styling: Kirsten Jones
Photography: Jerry Mucklow
Administration: Jim Baskett

Library of Congress Cataloging-in-Publication Data Available

10 9 8 7 6 5 4 3 2

First paperback edition published in 2003 by
Sterling Publishing Co., Inc.
387 Park Avenue South, New York, NY 10016

Produced by Prolific Impressions, Inc.
160 South Candler St., Decatur, GA 30030

© 2002 by Prolific Impressions, Inc.

Distributed in Canada by Sterling Publishing
C/o Canadian Manda Group, One Atlantic Avenue, Suite 105
Toronto, Ontario, Canada M6K 3E7
Distributed in Great Britain by Chrysalis Books Group PLC,
The Chrysalis Building, Bramley Road, London W10 6 SP, England.
Distributed in Australia by Capricorn Link (Australia) Pty. Ltd.
P.O. Box 704, Windsor, NSW 2756 Australia

Printed in China
All rights reserved

Sterling ISBN 0-8069-6863-X   Hardcover
           1-4027-0797-5   Paperback

Acknowledgments

Marie Browning would like to thank the following companies for their generous contributions of product, information, recipes and support:

Aquarius Aromatherapy & Soap
Mission, BC, Canada
www.aquariusaroma-soap.com
On-line suppliers of melt and pour soap bases, molds, fragrances, colorants, additives, inclusions, oils, packaging and information on all aspects of soap making.

Delta Technical Coatings
Whittier, CA
www.deltacrafts.com
Manufactures the "Soap Creations" line of melt and pour soap bases, molds, fragrances, cosmetic glitters, colorants and soap kits.

Environmental Technology, Inc.
Fields Landing, CA
www.eti-usa.com
Manufactures the "Fields Landing Soap Factory" line of melt and pour soap bases, including true coconut oil soap base, plastic tube molds, tray molds, fragrances, liquid cosmetic colorants and soap kits.

Image Hill
North Kansas City, MO
www.soapexpressions.com
Manufactures the "Soap Expressions" line of melt and pour soap bases, soap cubes, soap sheets, soap cutters, molds, fragrances, colorants, additives and soap kits.

Life of the Party
North Brunswick, NJ
www.soapplace.com
Manufacturer of melt and pour soap bases, molds, fragrances, colorants, additives and soap kits.

Martin Creative
Black Creek, BC, Canada
www.martincreative.com
High quality designer soap molds including two-part plastic tube molds.

Milky Way Molds
Portland, OR
www.milkywaymolds.com
High quality designer soap molds, soap stamps and two-part plastic tube molds.

Continued on next page

Sun Feather Natural Soap Company
Potsdam, NY
www.sunsoap.com
On-line suppliers of fine handcrafted soaps and soap making supplies, both cold process and melt and pour. Also lots of hard to find ingredients for soap making.

TKB Trading
Oakland, CA
www.tkbtrading.com
On-line suppliers of melt and pour soap bases, vegetable soap bases for hand milling, molds, fragrances, colorants, additives, inclusions, oils, and information on all aspects of soap making. TKB also manufactures high-quality soap colorants.

Yaley Enterprises, Inc.
Redding, CA
www.yaley.com
Manufactures the "Soapsations" line of melt and pour soap bases, molds, soap decal sheets, fragrances, and colorants.

About the Author

Marie Browning

Marie Browning is a consummate craft designer who has made a career of designing products, writing books and articles, and teaching and demonstrating. You may have been charmed by her creative acumen but not been aware of the woman behind it; she has designed stencils, stamps, transfers, and a variety of other products for art and craft supply companies.

300 Soap Recipes is her third book on soapmaking; the others are *Beautiful Handmade Natural Soaps* (Sterling, 1998) and *Melt & Pour Soapmaking* (Sterling, 2000). In addition to books about soapmaking, Browning has authored four other books published by Sterling: *Handcrafted Journals, Albums, Scrapbooks & More* (1999), *Making Glorious Gifts from Your Garden* (1999), *Hand Decorating Paper* and *Memory Gifts* (2000). Her articles and designs have appeared in *Handcraft Illustrated, Better Homes & Gardens, Canadian Stamper, Great American Crafts, All American Crafts,* and in numerous project books published by Plaid Enterprises, Inc.

Marie Browning earned a Fine Arts Diploma from Camosun College and attended the University of Victoria. She is a Certified Professional Demonstrator, a professional affiliate of the Canadian Craft and Hobby Association, and a member of the Stencil Artisans League and the Society of Craft Designers.

She lives, gardens, and crafts on Vancouver Island in Canada. She and her husband Scott have three children: Katelyn, Lena, and Jonathan. ❏

Contents

Introduction

Developing 300 different recipes for melt and pour soap was a challenge. I wanted to design different soaps that are practical as well as fun to make, and I had to keep it all organized in the process. I used 85 lbs. of melt-and-pour bases, over 160 different fragrances, 74 additives, 114 molds, 42 colorants, and 27 different techniques to come up with the selection you see here.

All the recipes are for **Melt & Pour Soap Making.** The recipes can also be used with *French-milled* soap making, with some adjustments. However, I chose to use only melt & pour techniques because of the availability of products and ease of techniques. Anyone can find the products needed and anyone can learn the easy techniques for making this type of soap. Certainly, my task was made easier by the wide range of products available and the willingness of the manufacturers to work with me. I'm grateful to the many soap crafters who shared their recipes and techniques and to my family, who offered up some great ideas. I made all the mistakes, perfected the techniques, and tested all the fragrance blends so that your creations will be successful. I hope your soap making experiences are enjoyable and rewarding.

Marie Browning

Supplies for Soap-Making

The ingredients and equipment needed for **Melt & Pour soapmaking** are readily available at stores that sell crafts supplies, grocery stores, health food stores, and drug stores and can be ordered from catalogs. Many items may already be in your kitchen. This section introduces and discusses the materials you'll need to make soap at home, including:

Soap Base

Fragrance

Additives

Colorant

Molds

Equipment

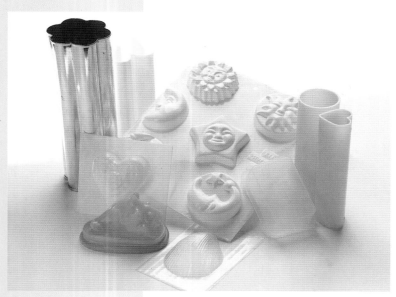

Melt and Pour Soap Base

There are many types of melt and pour soap bases available. The basic three are clear glycerin soap base, whitened glycerin soap base, and white coconut oil soap base. Soap base variations are the result of additives mixed into the bases, such as olive oil, coconut oil, hemp oil, and colorants. All melt and pour bases are designed to melt easily in the microwave or a double boiler and to be poured into molds.

People who are familiar with hand-milled and cold-processed soapmaking techniques will want to note these differences between those techniques and the melt-and-pour technique:

- Water is **never** added to melt and pour soap bases – it makes them slimy and prevents the soap from hardening properly.
- Melt and pour soaps set up immediately with little curing time, enabling you to create handmade soaps instantly.
- The creative and design possibilities are far greater with the melt and pour soap method.

Clear Glycerin Soap Base

High quality glycerin soap should be gentle enough for all skin types and have little scent (so it's ready for your own fragrant blends). If you wish a cloudy glycerin soap to be even more transparent when molded, simply melt, let harden, and re-melt before pouring into your mold. The second melting helps remove excess moisture from the soap. Most glycerin soaps have a melting point between 135 and 145 degrees F.

Whitened Glycerin Soap Base

Most white melt and pour bases are glycerin soap whitened with titanium dioxide, a white mineral pigment. They are sometimes called "coconut oil soap" when extra coconut oil is added. The soap has a milky translucent look when melted and a lower melting point. You can make your own whitened glycerin soap by adding white colorant to a clear soap base. Using the white colorant enables you to control the effects – you can add a little colorant for a translucent bar or more colorant for an opaque bar.

White Coconut Oil Soap Base

This base is true coconut oil soap, not just whitened glycerin soap with added coconut oil. Made with coconut and vegetable oils, this pH balanced soap is enriched with vitamin E and makes your skin feel soft, clean, and healthy. The coconut oil helps create a protective barrier that keeps the skin supple. It is easy to know if you are working with true coconut oil soap – when melted, it becomes clear; when fully hardened, it is a bright white soap. Coconut oil soap has a high melting point (190 degrees F.), which makes for a wonderful, hard-finished soap. This high temperature can melt some molds; make sure you cool the melted soap by stirring before pouring it into a mold.

Continued on next page

Other Glycerin Soap Bases

Most other soap bases are glycerin-based. Added ingredients provide different qualities. Some examples include:

- Glycerin with coconut oil - This soap base is an opaque white and may have a light coconut scent.
- Glycerin with avocado and cucumber - This opaque, pale green soap base has been enriched with vitamin E. A suspension formula keeps the additives uniformly distributed within the soap bar.
- Glycerin with olive oil - This soap base is a translucent natural amber or green color. The added olive oil hydrates the skin. It contains vitamin E and antioxidants and may feature a suspension formula.
- Glycerin with hemp oil - Silky and soothing, this translucent natural green-colored soap is good for dry skin and recognized for its ability to repair damaged skin cells.
- Glycerin with goat's milk - This opaque white soap base offers gentle moisturizing while maintaining the skin's natural pH level.
- Colored glycerin soap bases - These include clear colored soap bases, opaque colored soap bases, and bright florescent colored bases.
- Frosting soap base - A specialty soap base formulated to accent finished soaps, it has the look of fluffy white confectioner's icing.

Soap Base Forms

Soap bases come in different forms, including blocks and bars, soap sheets, pre-formed inserts (butterflies, stars, hearts, etc.), soap cubes, soap curls, soap noodles, and soap shavings.

Choosing Quality Melt and Pour Soap Bases

For best results and a high quality finished soap bar, purchase soap bases that are made with vegetable oils and without animal by-products or fillers such as wax and alcohol. The cheaper the soap, the more likely it is to contain wax and fillers. Wax and fillers are cheaper than other soap ingredients and account for the wide price ranges of melt and pour soap bases. Adding wax and fillers to glycerin soap base greatly diminishes the soap's cleansing qualities and lathering capabilities, and it can affect the smell and look of your finished soap.

Some melt and pour glycerin soap bases contain added alcohol as a means of removing moisture, thus making the soap more transparent. However, added alcohol creates a strong-smelling soap with several safety and health problems. Alcohol is very flammable and can ignite when the soap base is melted. Alcohol is also considered a skin irritant; repeated use will dry out your skin. Soap made with alcohol should not be used by anyone who has sensitive skin or dry skin.

Fragrance

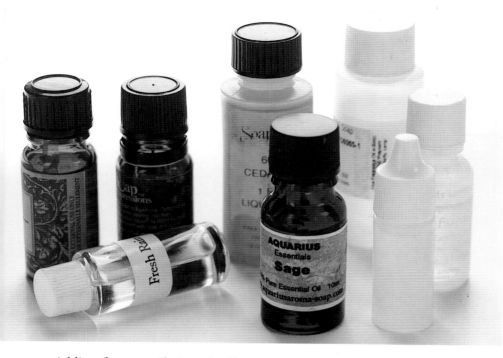

Fragrance Oil

Fragrance oils are much cheaper to produce than essential oils and are, therefore, less expensive. Since many fragrance oils are synthetic and are not derived from specific plants, they come in a much wider range of scents and blends than essential oils. Many high quality fragrance oils are actually blends of essential oils.

Continued on next page

Adding fragrant oils is a significant part of creating your soaps. Although some scents can come from additives, those scents will not be strong enough for a beautiful aromatic soap bar. The two main types of oils to use for soapmaking are essential oils – the fresh scents of flowers and herbs produced by plants – and fragrance oils, which are synthetically produced scents.

Fragrant oils are the most expensive ingredients you will buy, but they are the most important. I use both essential and synthetic fragrance oils in my soap recipes. Fragrance oils offer a wider selection of scents than would be obtainable if only essential oils were used.

Do not buy cheap oils or extracts – you will be disappointed in the finished product if you do. **Do not use** flavored extracts, potpourri oils, or candle scents in your soap projects – they are not safe to use on your skin.

Essential Oil

Of the many thousands of plants in the world, only 200 produce the aromatic essential oils used in the art of perfumery. Capturing the fragrance of flowers has been performed since ancient times for fragrance, healing, and mood altering qualities.

Essential oils are highly concentrated and must be diluted before they can safely be applied to the skin or blended into soaps (1% or less is considered to be a safe level for soapmaking). Too much essential oil can cause severe skin irritations. People with sensitive skin or allergies should be careful when using essential oils in their soap.

TIPS

Points to remember when adding fragrances to your products:

- In the recipes, I have used a moderate amount of fragrance oils for a nice, modest aroma. You may wish to add a little more for a stronger, more powerful scent.

- The amount of fragrance needed for each soap recipe varies, depending on the scent you select. Some oils are much stronger than others. Whatever the scent, make it stronger than you think, as some of it will dissipate.

- In this book, I refer to both essential and fragrance oils as fragrance oils. Let your budget and your nose dictate what oils to purchase. *Hint:* When buying fragrance oils, carry a bag of freshly ground coffee and sniff it occasionally to help clear your nose.

Your nose can help you determine the quality of a fragrance oil. Oils diluted (cut) with alcohol tend to smell alike and will have a sharp bite to them. Fragrance oils that contain alcohol adversely affect melt and pour soap bases – the alcohol pushes out moisture that forms white crystals on the soap.

Quality, uncut fragrance oils have a smooth, yet concentrated smell. When making soap, you will need to use more of a low quality fragrance oil than you would of a high quality fragrance oil to achieve the same results. Since less oil is required and the smell is often what invokes a positive response to a finished soap, good quality fragrance oils are a wise investment.

Basic Fragrance Blending

Fragrance blending is a centuries-old skill that creates bottles of luxury and dreams. Blending your own scents to create endearing and lasting fragrant blends is not difficult. Many soap recipes in this book use combinations of fragrance oils to create distinctive, enduring scents. The more oils you collect, the more experimenting and creating you can do.

Scents in the perfume trade are categorized into groups. Knowing these groups helps you decide how your blends will evolve; for example, you may want a rose scent (from the floral category) with a slight undertone of clove (from the spice category). You will naturally choose scents you find most appealing. While some people enjoy rich, earthy, exotic scents, others love the refreshing, clean scents of citrus or herbal categories.

The trend today is for single scented perfumes that smell like natural botanicals, such as a freshly sliced orange or a fresh sprig of peppermint. Though these perfumes smell like a single fruit, flower, or herb, they also contain other scents that make them lasting and more charming. The different scents, called "notes," are broken down into three main elements:

Main scent - The key or dominant scent in your blend. These high notes are the first aromas your nose detects.

Blenders - These additional scents enhance the main scent and form the middle notes of a blend.

Contrasting scents - These scents liven up the blend and provide the low notes that are the long-lasting scents.

FRAGRANCE GROUPS

The following is a partial list of fragrances and the scent groups to which they belong.

Citrus
Bergamot
Grapefruit
Lemon
Lemongrass
Lime
Mandarin
Pink grapefruit
Sweet orange
Tangerine

Spicy
Cinnamon
Clove
Ginger
Vanilla
Mixed spice blends

Herbal
Bayberry
Chamomile
Cucumber
Eucalyptus
Juniper
Peppermint
Pine
Rosemary
Sage
Tea tree

Fruity
Apricot
Blackberry
Blueberry
Coconut
Green apple

Kiwi
Mango
Melon
Mulberry
Pear

Floral
Jasmine
Lavender
Lilac
Lily of the valley
Plumaria
Rose
Violet
Ylang-ylang

Earthy
Amber
Frankincense
Honey
Musk
Patchouli
Sandalwood

Blended Fragrances
Baby powder
Brown sugar
Buttery maple
Candy cane
Chocolate
Honey almond
Ocean
Rain
Sunflower

Here's an example: The main scent is the overall aroma you wish to create, such as the tropical scent of coconut. The blender scent could be the floral notes of ylang-ylang that enhances and sweetens the main scent. The contrasting scent could be vanilla, which livens up the scent without overpowering the top two scents and provides the lasting note.

Points to consider when creating blends:
- *What's the fixative?* A fixative is necessary to help give the blend a long-lasting quality and release the fragrance moderately. The fixative takes the place of the plant's cells and holds the scent. It can be unscented or add its own aroma to the blend. In soap crafting, the fixative can be the soap base or dried botanical additives.
- *Test your fragrant blends* by placing a few drops of oil on a paper towel. Let the oils mingle for a few hours, then evaluate the blend by sniffing. Clear and refresh your sense of smell by sniffing a bag of freshly ground coffee from time to time when creating your blends.
- *Blender scents* - Some blends include scents from other categories. Successful blenders include lime, peppermint, lavender, rose, jasmine, sandalwood, vanilla, cinnamon, and honey.
- *Stay moist!* Dry skin does not hold fragrance as well as a skin that is well-hydrated.

Aromatherapy

Aromatherapy – the therapeutic use of oils derived from plants – is rooted in herbal medicine traditions that date back to prehistoric times. The ancient Egyptians, Greeks, Romans, and Hebrews were among the first to document the use of fragrances for cosmetic and medicinal purposes. It is the essential oil of a plant, often referred to as the plant's "soul" or "spirit," that is believed to affect our emotional, physical, and aesthetic well being.

Recently, aromatherapy has taken the cosmetics industry by storm, and many cosmetic firms have introduced an aromatherapy line that presents the beneficial aspects of fragrances. Although no medical claims can be made, it is certainly no surprise that a relaxing, scented bath can soothe us and renew our spirits.

Qualities Attributed to Essential Oils

Many essential oils have specific effects and qualities attributed to them. Below is a small sample of some of the most basic applications. Researchers are divided on whether the benefits of aromatherapy are conferred by the aromas or the other properties of the oils.

Peaceful and relaxing: Lavender, sandalwood, honeysuckle, chamomile, ylang-ylang, tangerine, rose, lemon verbena.

CAUTIONS

Essential oils are highly concentrated and potent substances, and it is important to understand a few cautionary guidelines when crafting with them.

- Do not take essential oils internally.
- Avoid all essential oils, natural herbal products, and salt baths during pregnancy.
- Essential oils should always be used diluted in a base; they are not perfumes that can be applied directly to your skin.
- Keep essential oils out of reach of children.
- Do not allow essential oils to come into contact with plastic. Certain oils will dissolve some plastics.
- Keep essential oils away from varnished or painted surfaces. For example, cinnamon oil can cleanly strip paint from furniture.

Energizing: Rosemary, peppermint, lemon, lime, jasmine, honey.
Stimulating and uplifting: Bergamot, orange, jasmine, rosemary, lemon verbena, mints, sage, pine.
Antiseptic: Tea tree, eucalyptus, peppermint, lavender.
Focusing, head-clearing: Frankincense, peppermint, grapefruit, cinnamon, chamomile, lavender, orange, ylang-ylang.

Additives for Soaps

Additives such as oatmeal, dried herbs, and oils can be added to soap bases to nourish, soften, and add gentle scrubbing properties. Additives used in soap can be found at grocery stores, health food stores, and craft supply outlets. Each ingredient offers its own unique characteristics to your products. Many additives also can add interesting colors and textures to your soap.

Remember these points when including additives in your soaps:

• **Always** use recommended safe ingredients. Just because an ingredient is natural, it doesn't mean it is safe to use in soap.

• Too much of an additive may soften your soap or make it scratchy and uncomfortable to use. Follow the recipe and use the recommended amount.

• Don't use fresh vegetables or fruits in melt and pour soap bases. Any material that is not properly dried or preserved can cause your soap to become rancid very quickly.

• Beware of soap recipes that include additives that make the soap look good but seem impractical or don't impart added benefits. For example, commercial potpourri may look good sprinkled in a clear soap, but the large petals will clog your drain and scratch your skin. Additionally, commercial potpourri may contain ingredients that would be dangerous to be in contact with your skin.

• When adding extra oils, add a natural preservative for a longer lasting bar. Natural preservatives include citric acid, vitamin E oil, and grapefruit seed extract.

SAFE ADDITIVES

Botanicals (dried)
Bergamot leaf and flower
Calendula petal
Chamomile blossoms
Coffee beans
Cranberries
Crushed apricots
Eucalyptus leaves
Ginger
Green tea
Kelp
Lavender buds
Lemon peel
Lemon verbena leaves
Lemongrass
Loofah
Orange peel
Peppermint leaves
Pine needles
Poppy seeds
Rose hips
Rose petals
Rosemary leaves
Sage leaves
Sandalwood
Strawberry leaf
Witch hazel (leaves and liquid extract)

Nuts
Almonds
Coconuts
Hazelnuts

Oils
Sweet almond oil
Cocoa butter
Coconut oil
Olive oil
Palm oil
Shea nut butter

Spices
Allspice
Anise
Cardamom
Cinnamon
Clove
Paprika
Tumeric
Vanilla pod

Miscellaneous
Aloe vera gel
Bee pollen
Cornmeal
French clay
Glycerin (liquid)
Honey
Milk (powdered whole cow's milk, goat's milk, and buttermilk)
Oatmeal
Oyster shell
Pumice
Rosewater
Salt (fine sea, rock)
Tapioca
Wheat bran

Preservatives
Citric acid
Grapefruit seed extract
Vitamin E (break open a capsule and squirt oil into melted soap)

A Few Cautions

Just because plants are natural doesn't mean that they are safe. Many of the world's deadliest poisons come from plants. Herbs must be used with caution, as many are potentially dangerous irritants or can cause allergic reactions. Almost every additive, natural or synthetic, can trigger someone's allergy or irritate someone's sensitive skin.

Although these reactions are annoying, it is possible to avoid a recurrence by eliminating the offending ingredient. You can perform a simple skin test to make sure you aren't allergic to a soap by rubbing a small amount of soap and water on the tender area on the inside of your elbow. If you are sensitive to any ingredient, your skin will develop redness or a slight rash.

- Avoid using soaps with abrasive fillers on your face. Save those soaps for rough spots such as elbows, knees, and hands. Soaps made from melt and pour soap bases that include essential oils and extra fats for moisturizing are best for cleansing your face.

- For natural additives, use the suggested ones. If you would like to explore this area further, there are many books available to educate you in the safe use of natural products.

- Use only herbs and flowers that are clean and free of insecticides and chemicals. Spray residues on plant material can irritate your skin. I prefer to use plants that I have grown myself. When this is not possible, purchase botanicals (ideally organically grown) from a natural food store or buy them fresh from the market and dry them yourself. Don't use dried botanicals from potpourri or dried flower arranging in soaps – these botanicals are not required to be food safe and may contain harmful dyes or chemicals.

- Cocoa butter, coconut oil, and almonds may produce a reaction in those allergic to chocolate and nuts.

- Natural emollients such as lanolin and glycerin may cause a reaction in those with sensitive skin.

- Honey, bee pollen, and beeswax may cause a reaction in those allergic to pollen. Do not use unpasteurized honey to scent products that will be used on infants.

TIPS

for Mixing Additives

- **Measuring and mixing.** Measure your additives and blend them before adding them to the melted soap.

- **Avoiding additive clumping.** Because additives such as powdered milk or spices can clump up, it's best to mix them with liquid glycerin before adding them to the melted soap base to help disperse them evenly.

- **Keeping additives on the surface.** Additives such as powdered spices, seeds, and grains will either sink to the bottom of the mold or float on the surface of the soap – an effect that can give the soap a natural, whimsical look. To achieve this effect, you can add the additives to the melted soap before pouring or place them in the bottom of the mold and pour the melted soap base on top.

- **Suspending additives.** To create a soap with additives suspended throughout, there are two options:

Option #1 – A special base. You can buy soap bases that have been especially formulated to suspend additives. If you use one of those, just add the additives, mix, and pour into the mold.

Option #2 – An extra step. After adding the additives to the melted soap base, gently stir the soap with a spoon to slowly cool and thicken the base. As soon as the soap starts to thicken, pour it into the mold. The soap will harden with the additives suspended throughout the soap. Be careful not to let the soap thicken so much that it won't pour. If this happens, re-melt and start again. *TIP:* I have found that, when mixing a large amount of soap, it's helpful to grate some of the same type of soap base and have a pile of it on hand to add to the soap – this will cool and quickly thicken the melted soap.

Colorant

Color Mixing Basics

The best way to learn about color mixing is through personal experience and experimentation. To get started, it helps to understand a few basic principles.

Color is an important ingredient of soap's allure. You can add spices and dried herbs for a natural soap or cosmetic grade colorants for a brightly colored bar.

Colorant Options

Soaps colored with natural powders have a wholesome, country look with attractive warm brown and tan hues. Some natural powders include cocoa powder, dried herbs, and ground spices.

Cosmetic grade colorants are available as both solids and liquids and can be found in the fragrance crafting departments of craft stores or from sellers of soapmaking supplies. High quality cosmetic grade colorants create true, clean colors and are excellent for blending and creating many different hues. The liquid colors come in red, blue, yellow, orange, green, white, and black. Solid colorants also are available in a wide range of hues.

For a sparkling effect, cosmetic grade glitters are available.

Don't Use Food Coloring

Food coloring is not suitable for soapmaking – the color quickly fades. Food coloring also is not suitable for bath oil; the dyes are not soluble in oil and just sit on top as floating beads of concentrated color. You can, however, use small amounts of food coloring to color bath salts and bubble bath.

Primary colors are red, blue, and yellow. *Secondary colors* are mixes of primary colors – green (yellow + green), purple (red + blue), and orange (red + yellow). *Intermediate colors* are mixes of a primary color with a neighboring secondary color on a color wheel; e.g., lime green, which is a mixture of yellow + green.

Complementary colors are colors that are opposite one another on the color wheel – red is the complement of green, purple is the complement of yellow, blue is the complement of orange. When you mix a color with its complement; the result is a dulling or muting of the color, making it less intense.

Here are some examples:
• Dusty plum - Purple + a touch of its complement, yellow
• Golden ocher - Yellow + a touch of its complement, purple

Shades are made by adding black to a color. *Tints* are made by adding white.

Equipment & Tools

The basic equipment and tools for creating melt and pour soaps are standard kitchen items that you possibly already own.

Glass Measuring Cups - Use heat-resistant glass measuring cups to melt soap bases in the microwave or on the stovetop (with a pan to make a double boiler). You need 1-cup, 2-cup, and 4-cup sizes.

Measuring Spoons - You need a set of metal or plastic measuring spoons for measuring additives.

Glass Droppers - You will need three to five glass droppers for measuring fragrance oils. **Do not use plastic droppers.** They can't be cleaned completely (so you could contaminate your oils with other scents), and some essential oils will dissolve the plastic!

Electric Spice/Coffee Grinder - A small electric grinder is useful when grinding small amounts of additives, such as spices, almonds, or oatmeal. Clean the grinder after each use by grinding a piece of fresh bread or some rice (the bread or rice soaks up oils), then wipe with a paper towel.

Mortar and Pestle - I often prefer to use a mortar and pestle for grinding rather than an electric grinder – I find I have more control. A mortar is easier to clean, too – just wipe it out with a paper towel after use.

Mixing Spoons - Metal or wooden kitchen spoons are needed to mix melted soap. Since metal spoons will not transfer fragrances, they are safe for food use after cleaning. If you use wooden spoons, clearly mark them FOR FRAGRANCE CRAFTING ONLY and don't use them for food – the wood will retain scents and transfer them to your food.

Large Saucepan *(for the stovetop method)* - You will need a large saucepan; any metal is fine. Use the pan to make a simple double boiler – put water in the saucepan and place a large heat-resistant glass measuring cup in it for melting the soap bases.

Paper Cups - Use small paper cups to hold pre-measured additives and to use as equal size risers for tray molds that will not sit level on a flat surface.

Sharp Knife - Use a sharp knife to cut blocks of melt and pour soap base into smaller pieces and to slice your finished molded soaps. Having a variety – from small paring knives to large butcher knives – is handy.

Wax Paper - Use wax paper to protect your work area when pouring and molding soaps.

Soap Beveller - This is really a cheese planer that can be used to bevel soap edges. It can also be used to clean soap surfaces and make wonderful soap curls.

Kitchen Tools - Many kitchen tools come in handy for special effects. A melon baller can be used to scoop out uniform holes from soap; a garnish cutter can be used to slice soaps with a decorative wavy cut.

Caring for Tools & Equipment

Clean glass and metal tools thoroughly after use. After cleaning, they can be used for food preparation. Plastic and wood items used for soap-making should **not** be used for food.

Molds

Molds Especially for Soapmaking

High heat plastic soap molds are, overall, the best and safest for soapmaking. Their deep, clean, smooth contours allow you to create professional looking soaps safely and unmold them easily. The molds come in individual shapes or in trays of fancy motifs. They are designed to last through repeated moldings and will withstand the high temperatures of melt and pour soap bases without warping or melting. Good quality soap molds don't require pre-treatment to release the hardened soaps and are self-leveling. Large soap loaf molds are available in a variety of sizes and shapes. Look for very small shapes designed especially for chunk-style soaps at crafts stores.

Tube molds are available in plastic and metal, in both tubular and two-part, snap-together styles. Having a selection of large and small tube molds in basic shapes enables you to make a wide selection of designs. They also have other crafting and culinary uses.

Individual resin casting molds are an excellent size and depth for single bars of homemade soap. The number of ounces of melted soap the mold holds is printed into the bottom of each mold.

Molds help you make your melt and pour soaps appear more professional and fancy. It's a good idea to have a selection of soap molds that includes traditional soap shapes and fun theme shapes.

Most molds can tolerate temperatures of 135 to 145 degrees F. Over-heated soap sometimes warps even the best soap molds. This can happen especially with coconut oil soap, which has a high melting point (190 degrees F.). To avoid warping, cool the soap by stirring or set the molds in a shallow cold-water bath for high temperature pours.

Mold designs show up clearer and crisper in hard soap than in soft soap. Adding palm oil or cocoa butter can harden soft glycerin soaps.

Caution: Be careful when choosing plastic containers for molding your soaps. Some cannot take the high temperature of the melted soap and can melt and collapse, causing a spill.

Candle Molds

Some **plastic candle molds** are suitable for soapmaking. Since candle molds are designed to withstand the high temperatures of melted wax, they can withstand hot soap without melting. It can be difficult, however, to unmold the soap. For best results, choose low, wide molds rather than long, skinny ones and *always* use a mold release.

Metal candle molds can handle the high temperatures, but most soap chemically reacts with metal, especially aluminum. This reaction causes the metal to corrode, and the corrosion discolors your soap and will eventually destroy your metal molds. Because they are rigid, metal molds need a mold release.

Rubber Latex Molds

Rubber latex molds make beautiful three-dimensional soaps. (Rubber molds for candlemaking also can be used.) Because red rubber flexible molds can transfer the color to the soap, choose amber colored rubber molds.

You can also make your own rubber molds, using a liquid rubber mold builder that takes an impression of a wide selection of objects. Imagine using a shell, glass figurine, or stone carving to make your own signature soap mold!

Plastic Food Storage Containers

Small sandwich or storage containers (4" x 6") will accommodate loaf-style soaps. Try to find ones with no design on the inside bottom and with nicely rounded corners. **CAUTION:** Some plastic containers cannot withstand the high temperature of melted soap base and will melt and collapse, spilling the hot soap. Look for containers that are dishwasher and microwave safe; be wary of disposable plastic containers and takeout food containers, which are intended for one-time use and are not as sturdy. When using plastic containers, *always* stir the soap before pouring to cool it.

Candy and Plaster Molds

Plaster and candy molds can warp, as they cannot take the high temperatures of the melt and pour soap. If hot melted soap is poured into them, they melt or de-form; spilling their contents and resulting in serious burns if one is not careful. Many plastic molds designed to keep food from crushing are tempting because of the wonderful designs and deep shapes, but the plastic will warp and melt when the soap is added. For this reason, many plastic cups are unsuitable for soapmaking.

Mold Releases

To help the soap release from the mold, I prefer to coat the mold with a thin layer of petroleum jelly before pouring in the soap. Widely used in cosmetics as an emollient and barrier cream, petroleum jelly does not leave a sticky residue on the soap.

Another suggestion for a soap release comes from the manufacturer of Milky Way soap molds: Melt one part (by weight) paraffin wax and stir in three parts baby oil. This is best used when hot, but it can be applied when cold as a soft paste. Make sure you have thin, even application, or it can mar the smoothness of the finished soap.

Vegetable oil in liquid and spray forms is also used as a mold release. However, I don't recommend it because even with a thin film on the mold, it tends to make the soap a bit greasy and the oil can turn rancid over time, altering the fragrance of the soap.

UNMOLDING TIPS

- *Use gentle pressure.* release the soap from tray molds by using gentle pressure from your thumbs on the back of the mold. You can easily damage molds with improper handling.

- *Leave it in the mold.* If the soap is allowed to remain in the mold for 12-24 hours after cooling down, it will release much more easily than if unmolded immediately upon cooling.

- *Try the freezer.* If you still find it difficult to release the soap from a mold, try placing it in the freezer for 10 minutes, remove, and try again.

Melt & Pour Technique

PREPARATION TIPS

- To calculate the amount of soap needed to fill your mold, fill the mold with water, then pour the water in a measuring cup to measure.

- Always melt at least one additional ounce of soap to account for the soap that will cling to the inside of the measuring cup.

- Slice the soap base into small pieces for quick, easy melting.

- Make sure all the bowls, measuring cups, and mixing spoons are completely dry.

- **Never add water** to melt and pour soap bases.

1 Place the soap into a heat-resistant glass measuring cup and microwave for approximately 30 seconds to 1 minute on high for approximately 1 cup of soap pieces. The melting time will vary depending on the amount of soap and the type of soap. It is much better to melt the soap in small time intervals to keep the soap from boiling over.

2 Remove from the microwave and stir lightly to completely melt any remaining soap pieces. Do not leave the mixing spoon in the soap while heating in the microwave or when melting on the stovetop.
Melting Option: You also can melt the soap in a double boiler on the stove. Adjust the heat to keep the soap at a constant liquid point. Do not let soap heat for more than 10 minutes.

3 Immediately add any additives or coloring to the melted soap and stir gently to mix. If the soap starts to solidify, reheat it to re-melt it.

4 Add the drops of fragrance oil until desired level of fragrance is achieved.

5 Pour the soap into the mold immediately after the fragrance is added.

6 Let the soap cool and harden completely before removing from the mold. The soap will pop out easily when completely set. For a fast set, allow the soap to set in the refrigerator until cooled.

TIPS

• It is harmless to re-melt the soap. If you melt more soap base than what fills your chosen mold, pour the extra soap base into a spare mold or plastic container, let harden, release, and re-melt for another project. (It's a good idea to always have an extra mold on hand in case this happens.)

• Repeated re-melting of clear glycerin soap base makes it more transparent, as the excess moisture evaporates. Repeated re-melting of coconut oil soap base makes the resulting soap harder.

• When cleaning up, don't put your measuring cups or spoons in the dishwasher. Soap base is designed to make lots of luxurious bubbles, and the soap left on the equipment could foam and cause the dishwasher to leak. Roll up your sleeves and wash the few pieces of equipment by hand.

• Experimenting by trial and error helps you understand the process.

Hand-Milled Soap Technique

Converting Recipes for Hand-Milled Soapmaking

Hand milled (also called re-batching or French milling) is a soap making process that is quite different from the melt and pour technique of soap making. This method starts by grating a pre-made soap bar, melting it with water and adding beneficial additives, fragrances and oils to produce superior quality soap. Hand milled soaps usually take up to 2 - 4 weeks to cure before using, where melt and pour soaps can be used immediately. Unlike melt and pour soaps to which you do not add water or fresh ingredients, hand milling allows you to add properly preserved fresh ingredients for unique finished soaps. A few suggested ingredients you can add include carrot juice, cucumbers,

Comparison of Melt and Pour soap making and Hand-milled soap making:

HAND-MILLED

Soap Base	Method	Curing	Molding
Start with a pre-made soap bar, preferably a vegetable based soap made with the cold process method. You can also use high quality purchased soap bars. This technique is a more economical method to produce your own soap bars.	The soap is grated and melted with water in a double boiler on the stove-top. Soap makers have also used crockpots to melt the soap. Fresh preserved additives, oils, fragrances, dried botanicals and colorants can all be added to create the soap bars.	The soap sometimes requires up to 4 weeks to completely cure, but in most cases can be used within 2 weeks of making. Hand milled soaps can be packaged without wrapping in plastic wrap and the bars become harder and better the longer they cure.	Use simple shaped soap molds with large embossed decorations. Hand milling is my preferred method for hand molded natural looking soap balls. You are limited to the different techniques you can achieve with this method, but it is an excellent way to produce natural looking soap bars.

MELT & POUR

Soap Base	Method	Curing	Molding
The soap base is specially formulated to melt easily in your microwave. The bases come in a variety of types including clear glycerin and white coconut oil and with added ingredients such as olive oil, goat's milk and hemp oil. This method is more expensive than hand milling but the time to make the bars is greatly reduced.	The soap base is cut into small pieces to melt quickly in you microwave. Water and fresh ingredients are not added to the melt and pour soap base. Fragrances, oils, additives and colorants can all be added to create the soap bars. Easy enough to do with children with adult supervision.	The soap is ready to use right after it comes out of the mold. Because of the high moisture content in melt and pour soaps it is wrapped in plastic to keep fresh. The soap is best used within three months of making as the fragrance fades and the colorants migrate	Many decorative, designer-like techniques can be done with this method. The clear glycerin soap allows you to embed treasures and add decorative additives such as soap glitters. The new tube soaps allow for fast and easy designer soaps and tray molds can be very detailed with this method.

avocados, bananas or strawberries. For more information on this process refer to "Natural Soapmaking" by Marie Browning, Sterling Publications.

Many of the "natural" soap recipes in this publication can be converted to the hand-milling process following these simple procedures and tips:

• Use the fragrance blends, additives and colorants from the recipes for converting to the hand milled process.

• Remember that the hand milled soap method does not produce clear, translucent bars like the clear glycerin melt and pour soap base.

• Many of the decorative treatments such as chunk style soaps, tube mold soaps, and some embedded soap techniques are unsuitable for the hand milled method.

• Decorative treatments such as soap beads, some embedded soaps, painted soaps, carved soaps and decoupaged soaps are suitable for hand milled soaps.

• For each melted ounce of melt and pour soap base substitute an ounce of melted soap in the hand-milled process. This is a very general substitution; a little more or less will not affect the outcome of the finished bar.

• Molds should be simple shapes and free of intricate designs. Treat molds with a mold release such as petroleum jelly (Vaseline® brand).

• Double the fragrance amount in the recipe as some of the fragrance will dissipate during the curing process.

• Keep the added botanicals and oils the same amount as stated in the recipes when applying it to hand-milled soap making.

• Keep the colorants the same amount as stated in the recipes when applying it to hand-milled soap making.

• The additives, colorants and fragrances are added after the soap has been melted and just before pouring into the molds.

General Directions for hand-milled soap making:

1. Grate and process until fine, 2 cups vegetable based soap.
2. Place grated soap in a heat resistant glass measuring bowl.
3. Add any oil that the recipe calls for. Add 1/3-cup water.
4. Place measuring bowl in a hot water bath on the stovetop. Melt the soap, stirring gently until the soap starts to appear "stringy".
5. Remove the melted soap from the heat and add the additional ingredients. Stir the mixture to disperse the ingredients.
6. Working quickly, spoon or pour into the prepared mold.

CAUTIONS

• Be careful when working with melted soap. It can be very hot and can burn your skin if you spill it on you. Melt and pour soap bases are especially hot when melted (up to 190 degrees F.). If you do spill hot melted soap on your skin, place the exposed area in cold water immediately. Overheating the soap base in the microwave can cause the soap base to boil and overflow the cup and spill over on your hand. Heat the soap in brief intervals to prevent overheating. Keep melted soap away from children.

• Spilled soap or oil can make floors slippery and cause dangerous falls. If you accidentally spill liquid soap or oil while working, clean it up immediately. The soap will solidify quickly – scrape it up and rinse the area well.

• Clearly label any porous fragrance crafting tools, such as wooden spoons and plastic molds, so they won't be used in food preparation. Glass items are safe to use as they do not retain scents and residues.

• Clearly label your finished products with their contents and instructions for use. Some soaps look and smell so yummy that someone may mistake them for food!

Designer Techniques

Chunk Style Soaps

This double-molded method suspends colored pieces of a soap in a larger block of clear or opaque soap. The added pieces (soap #1) can be molded, slivered into long curls, cut into chunks, or grated before it is added to the mold and the soap #2 is poured in. It is best to chill the pieces for adding in a refrigerator for 10 minutes before pouring the hot soap to prevent the pieces from melting. Examples of chunk style soaps are Recipe #49 Green Tea Cardamom, Recipe #84 Byzantine Mosaic, and Recipe #289 Rainbow Loaf.

You will make more successful chunk style soaps if all the soap pieces are of the same type base. If you add coconut oil chunks to a glycerin soap, for example, the resulting bar will fall apart because the two bases dry at different rates.

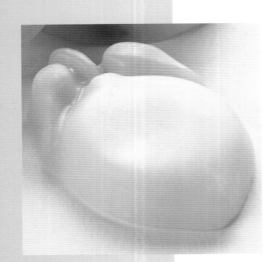

Soaps with Defined Colored Areas

You can create multi-colored soaps by double molding different colors and types of soap. For example, to make a checkered soap, you first mold soap in one color (soap #1), cut the soap into squares, and arrange the squares in the mold in a checkerboard pattern. Chill the pieces in the refrigerator for 10 minutes, then pour the second color soap (soap #2) on top. These soaps differ from chunk style soaps in that the pieces of soap #1 are arranged to create a specific pattern or motif. An example is #140 - Whimsical Checkered.

Another example of this technique is Recipe #58 Summer Lemon, a yellow lemon with green leaves. To make it, I poured yellow soap base in a lemon-shaped mold. After releasing the soap, I trimmed off the leaves and placed the lemon piece back in the mold. After chilling the piece, I poured in green soap base so the leaves would be green.

Molds with a raised or embossed motif on one side can be used to make a beautiful bar with a well-defined, different-colored motif on top. Pour soap #1 in the embossed area. Let harden, then pour a contrasting color soap base on top. There usually is no need to chill the mold before pouring the second soap base. Examples of this technique include #81 Aegean and #89 Celtic Heart Knot.

For a perfect combination bar, use this "pour-and-scrape" technique: Pour soap #1 in the embossed area. Let it harden a bit, then take a piece of hard plastic (an old credit card works great!) and scrape away any soap that spilled over and out of the embossed design area. Then pour in soap #2. Examples are #229 Tranquility and #218 Dreaming.

Marbled Soaps

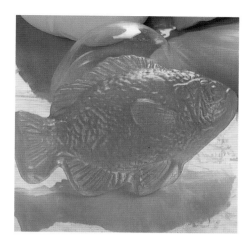

You can make beautiful marbled soaps by pouring clear glycerin and whitened glycerin soap bases into a mold at the same time and letting them gently swirl together. Melt the different soaps at the same time and, for best results, stir the soap and let it cool and thicken slightly before pouring. You can color the soaps if you like.

You can also use the same technique to pour two colors of coconut oil soap base. *Don't* pour white coconut oil soap base and clear glycerin soap base together to create a marbled effect – they will separate because of their different densities. Examples of marbled soaps are #259 Marbled Sea Shells and #262 Lena's Blue Fish.

Layered Soaps

Making layers with the same soap base: The most successful layered soaps are made from different colors of the same soap base. Simply let the first layer harden before pouring the next layer. Be sure the melted soap is hot enough to stick to the cured soap but not so hot that it makes the cured soap melt.

Making layers with different soap bases: Since white coconut oil soap base and clear glycerin soap base separate when poured together due to their different densities, the two bases can be used to create layered soaps – the glycerin soap base sinks, the white coconut oil base rises to the top, and there's a mixed layer in between.

Samples of layered soaps are #255 Purple Crystal, #288 Harlequin, and #249 Sedimentary Layered.

ABOUT USING ALCOHOL

Many books – but not mine – recommend you spray alcohol on soap pieces when making chunk style or layered soaps to help the soap adhere. I have tested this technique repeatedly, and my experience says it doesn't work. I find soap pieces do not fall out of my finished soaps and last longer in the bath when I have not used alcohol. (One exception: When a soap base contains extra alcohol, this technique works to a small extent, but you also add more drying properties to your soap, which is undesirable.)

I also never spray alcohol on the top of the soap to remove bubbles. I prefer to wait until a skin forms; I then carefully remove the skin with a knife. You can also trim off the bubbles that form on a hardened soap bar by planing the soap with a soap beveller.

Tube Molded Soaps

Tubular loaf-style molds come in different styles, designs, and sizes. Small, medium, and large molds make for endless design possibilities! The basic technique involves placing smaller soap columns in larger tube molds to create a variety of designs that last the life of the soap. The smaller columns are first molded in a smaller tube mold, released then placed in the larger molds. The tube molds can also be used alone, without placing a smaller column inside. Designs can be as simple as a small star in a larger star or more complicated. Samples of this technique include #22 Cucumber Mint, #133 Orange Slice.

The recipes in this book make two to three bars, which is a good way to learn the technique before making larger batches that fill the molds completely. One advantage of using a vertical tube mold over a horizontal loaf mold is that you can pour one, two, or three inches of soap in the tube mold rather than having to fill the entire mold. This is a great way to use up small bits of soap and make small batches.

Helpful Hints for Successful Tube Molded Soaps

• **Use clear glycerin soap base.** I have found clear glycerin soap base is the best type for tube-molded soaps – the soaps won't fall apart when you use them. The tube mold recipes in this book use clear glycerin soap base for all moldings. For a white or opaque hue, add white colorant to clear base.

• **Use a mold release.** Coat tube molds (both plastic and metal) with a thin layer of petroleum jelly on the inside to aid in releasing the soap.

• **Prepare the mold.** You must prepare the tube mold **every time** you use it. Failure to prepare the mold (even if it comes with a cap on the bottom) will result in soap leaking out of the mold and running all over your work area. Here's how:

1. Cover the bottom of the tube mold with four layers of plastic wrap. Secure with a rubber band.

2. Pour 1/2" of melted soap base in the mold to create a plug at the bottom. Let harden, then pour the soap in the mold.

TIP: Place the prepared mold in a small plastic container. That way, if your mold does leak, the soap will be safely contained and can be easily re-melted. You will also be able to move the mold after pouring the soap.

• **To make small dots in soap designs:**

1. Prepare the mold and let the soap plug at the bottom harden.
2. Push plastic straws into the plug.
3. Pour melted soap base in the mold around the straws. Let harden completely.
4. Remove the straws without releasing the soap. Pour the desired color of melted soap in the holes. Let harden, then proceed.

• **Arranging with chopsticks:** When using small soap pieces in large tube molds, a pair of chopsticks comes in handy for moving and arranging the pieces. Don't worry about getting the placement perfect, the soaps are designed to be whimsical.

• **Tips for defined color areas:** When pouring soap #2 in and around smaller soap pieces of soap #1, stir soap #2 after melting to cool it a bit before pouring in the mold. You can also place the pieces of soap #1 in the refrigerator for 10 minutes before putting them in the mold. The smaller the soap columns you place in a large mold, the greater chance of the pieces melting.

Removing Soaps from Tube Molds

Let the soap cool and harden completely before attempting to push it out of the mold. Hardening times will vary, depending on the size of the mold and the amount of soap base.

1. Remove the plastic wrap from the bottom.
2. Place a crumpled paper towel into the mold (this prevents damage to the soap) and push the soap from the mold.

TIPS

for Unmolding

- Use a smaller tube mold to push out soap from a larger tube mold.

- For smaller molds (the hardest molds to release), place a piece of crumpled paper towel or a coin on the soap and use a wooden dowel or unsharpened pencil to push out the hardened soap.

- **Never** use a knife, fork, or other sharp utensil to push out the soap – you could seriously injure yourself or damage the soap.

- If the soap won't push out, place the tube mold in the refrigerator for 10 minutes. The soap should come out easily.

For Slicing

- Use a large knife to slice your tube of soap into bars. Soap made in the smaller molds can be sliced 1/2" thick; soap made in medium and large molds can be cut 3/4" to 1" thick.

- Large circular and rectangular tube molds can be cut in half to create half circle or smaller rectangular bars.

Soap Beads

Smaller tube molds make great soap "beads" for the Soap Tassel™ recipes. Simply pour the colored, fragrant soap base into a prepared mold. Let set and release. Cut into slices 1" thick. Thread thin satin ribbon through the eye of a large darning needle and thread on the "beads."

Stacked Shapes

Soap sheets are used to make stacked soap shapes. Examples of this technique are Recipe #149 Stars and Recipe #150 Flowers.

Soap sheets are great for children to craft with, as there is no hot, melted soap to worry about. Soap sheets can be purchased or you can make your own. Here's how:
1. Line cookie sheets with wax paper.
2. Prepare the soap base and pour a small amount on the wax paper-lined cookie sheets. It will spread. (You want the soap to be 1/4" thick.) Let cool completely.

You can cut the soap sheets with cookie cutters. To adhere the cutout shapes, use a hair dryer to slightly melt the top of the soap sheet cutout before placing another cutout on top. *Option:* Melt some clear glycerin soap base. Pour a small amount on the top of the cutout shape and place the second piece on top. The melted soap "glues" the pieces together.

Embedded Soaps

Embedded soaps have an object or item – such as a toy or a sponge or a saying on a piece of laminated paper, referred to as the "embed" – placed in the mold. The soap base is poured around the embed.

- **Soaps with Embedded Sponges:** Loofahs or small sponges can be added to float on the freshly poured melted soap (#208 Spa Therapy) or placed in the mold before the soap is added (#141 Natural Loofah Rounds). The sponges should be dry before they are added to the soap.
- **Embedded Toy Soaps:** Soaps with embedded toys are fun and whimsical. I use a first layer of clear glycerin soap (so the toy can be seen) and a second layer of colored whitened glycerin soap that contrasts with the color of the toy. Examples are #153 Happy Face Treasure and #157 Dino in a Dino. You can also add soap glitter to the second layer for sparkle.

Choose safe, soft toys; don't use anything that is sharp or has points. **CAUTION: Soaps with small toys should not be given to children under three years of age.**

I have made many toy embedded soaps. This technique is my favorite.
1. Pour a small amount of melted clear glycerin soap in the mold. Wait until a skin forms on the top. Carefully remove the skin with the point of a knife. (This removes any bubbles or foam from the top of the soap.)
2. While the soap is still liquid, add the toy *face down* to the mold. Let harden.
3. Pour in more melted soap to fill the mold.

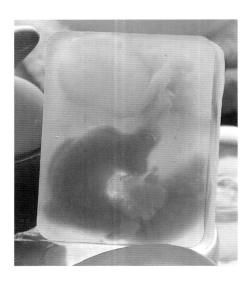

Soaps in Soap

You can mold small soaps and embed them into a clear soap bar to make a soap within a soap. Examples are #160 Ocean Motifs and #162 Funky Lemon. Here's how:

1. Make the small soaps. Let cool and harden, then remove from the molds.
2. Chill the small soaps in the refrigerator for 10 minutes.
3. Follow the instructions for "Embedded Toy Soaps."
4. Soap curls, soap noodles, and soap cubes also can be arranged and embedded in a clear soap base – just arrange the small soap pieces in a mold and cool in the refrigerator before pouring the hot melted soap over them in the mold. An example of this technique includes #171 Cucumber Peel.

Decorative Accents

Instead of embedding soap pieces, add them to the top of the soap bar. Melt a little clear glycerin soap base and use it as glue to adhere the pieces. See #106 Honeysuckle Blossom.

You can also accent a soap bar with a whole spice or toy. (It will come off with the first use.) An example is #65 Witch Hazel Anise. Here's how:

1. Make a small hole on the top of the soap.
2. Melt a small amount of clear glycerin soap base. Pour it in the hole.
3. Place the accent on top of the melted soap in the hole.
4. Pour the melted soap base over the entire bar and accent.

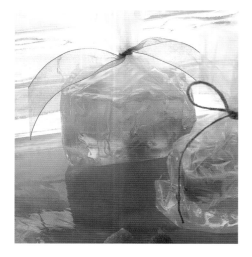

Bagged Soaps

These soaps are molded in a plastic bag that is the package for the presentation. Examples are #163 Jellies and #166 Candy Hearts. Here's how to make them:

1. Fill a plastic bag with soap pieces.
2. Place in the refrigerator for 10 minutes to cool.
3. Place the cooled bag of soap in a 3" tube mold. (This holds it upright.)
4. Pour clear, scented soap base in the bag. Be sure to use fragrance oil that does not impart color to the clear soap base. Let the soap set.
5. Tie a ribbon to close the bag for presentation. To use, simply peel back the plastic bag.

Basic Recipe
Solid Fizzy Bath Salts

1 cup sodium bicarbonate (baking soda)

3/4 cup citric acid

1/4 cup binder

20 drops fragrance oil

5 drops liquid colorant

Instructions

1. Mix all the dry ingredients in a large glass bowl, using your hands to break up any lumps.

2. Remove approximately 1/2 cup of the mixed dry ingredients and place in a small bowl.

3. Add the coloring and fragrance oils to the small bowl and mix well with the dry ingredients. Use a spoon at first, then mix with your hands to get the coloring and fragrance evenly distributed throughout the dry ingredients.

4. Place the colored, fragrant mix from the small bowl back in the large bowl. Mix well.

5. Spritz the salts lightly with a fine mist of water and immediately mix with your hands. CAUTION: **Do not** over-mist or your salts will start to fizz up! Continue misting lightly and mixing until the salts just hold together.

6. Follow the individual recipes for molding the salts around the soap pieces.

7. Let dry overnight until hard.

Fizzy Soaps

Fizzy soaps are small soaps encased in solid fizzy bath salts. When a fizzy soap is placed in the tub, the salts fizz away, scenting and softening the water, and reveal the small soap bar, which has a matching scent. Examples are #167 English Rose and #168 Chocolate Tub Truffle.

Embossed Soaps

You can use plastic toys, rubber stamps, or soap stamps to emboss your soaps. Plastic toys, used for the Fossil Soaps described below, and rubber stamps are placed before molding the soap. Soap stamps are used after the soap is molded and released.

Fossil Soaps

This technique is courtesy of Environmental Technologies and was developed by my good friend Jan Ryan-Moore. We were both making soap one day and, while experimenting with the embedding process, discovered plastic toys leave a detailed impression in the finished soap. It was Jan who saw the possibilities of this and exclaimed "You better give me credit for this in your next book!" Examples include #69 Fish Fossil Soap. Here's how:

1. Line a mold with aluminum foil. (This gives a natural stone look to the finished soap.)

2. Glue a plastic toy face up in the bottom of the mold with rubber cement. (If you don't glue it, it just floats to the top.)

3. Pour in the melted soap base, let harden, then release. If the toy sticks to the soap, carefully use a knife to help remove it from the soap.

Rubber Stamp Embossed Soaps

You can also use a deeply etched rubber stamp (with the base removed) to emboss a soap bar. Examples include #90 - Celtic and #235 Classic Embossed. Here's how:

1. Carefully peel the stamp from the wooden base. *TIP:* Place the stamp in the microwave for 20 seconds to help it come apart easily.

2. Glue the stamp, right side up, in the bottom of a mold with rubber cement. (Rubber cement won't harm the mold or the stamp.

3. Pour the soap in the mold and let set.

4. Remove the soap from the mold. (The rubber stamp usually comes out with the soap.)

5. Use a corsage pin to carefully pry the stamp from the hardened soap.

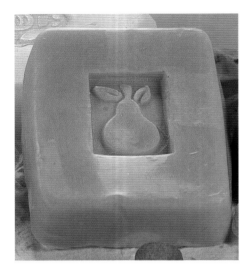

Soap Stamps

You can buy beautiful stamps especially made for embossing soaps. Using an embossing stamp is quicker than using rubber stamps for embossing if you are planning to do more than one bar of soap. An example is #237 Pear Embossed. Here's how:

1. Mold the soap and release from the mold.
2. Right away, place the soap on a hard, level surface. Position the embossing stamp on the soap and pound the back of the stamp with a hammer to make the impression in the soap.

Painted Soaps

Painting is a wonderful way to personalize and add your own designs to soaps. **Always** choose paints that are specially formulated to work and be safe on soap. Soap paints come in colors or as a clear medium that you mix with acrylic paints. Use the colored paints straight from the bottle (**don't** thin with water). If using the clear soap medium, mix equal amounts medium and acrylic paint. Use a brush, sponge, or toothpick to apply the paint. Clean up with soap and water. Here are some soap painting ideas:

• *Dip-Dot Painting* - Add designs to your soap with simple paint dots applied with a toothpick. Use the dots to accent a stenciled design (see #73 Australian Spirit) or make a floral design (see #179 Dip-Dot Rose).

• **Stenciling:** Use purchased stencils to accent your soaps. Use a very small amount of paint for stenciling. Remove excess paint from the brush before stenciling by blotting the brush on a paper towel. *TIP:* If the paint leaks under the stencil, you are using too much paint! If this happens, simply wipe the paint off the soap with a paper towel and start again. Stenciling examples are #72 Stone Age Ritual and #79 Egyptian Musk.

• **Dry Brushing:** You also can apply soap paint with a dry brush technique – simply remove excess paint from your brush with a paper towel before painting the soap. Examples are #88 Raphael Angel and #114 - Folk Art Heart.

• **Adding accents and highlights:** You can highlight the raised area of an embossed or stamped soap bar by dry brushing with soap paint or by rubbing on a small amount of gold luster powder. An example is #62 Mandarin Spice.

Carved & Cut Soaps

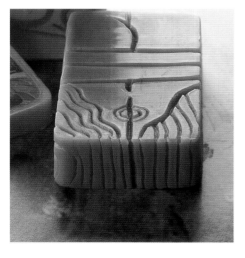

Soap carving is an easy and fun way to accent a bar. Use a small sharp knife without serrated edges to carve a design or whittle the soap into a new shape. Trimming edges with a soapbeveller is another carving technique that gives a soap bar a professional finish. Carved soap examples include #103 Kiss, #183 Carved Soap on a Rope, and #239 Amethyst.

You can also use a melon baller or other kitchen tools to cut soap into shapes. An example is #191 Funky Dots.

Decoupaged Soap

You can easily decoupage cut motifs from patterned tissue paper or paper napkins to the soap bar with clear soap medium. An example is #80 Ancient Shard. Here's how:

1. Cut out the paper motif.
2. Brush a layer of medium on the soap.
3. Add the paper design.
4. Brush a second layer of medium over the cutout.
5. *Optional:* The paper will come off during the first use of the soap. To make the design last the life of the soap, dip the decoupaged side of the bar in melted paraffin wax.

Decals on Soap

Decals especially made for soap are available for decorating your soaps, and the images will not wash out. Decals look best on white or light colored soap bars. An example is #267 Christmas Guest Bars. Here's how to add decals:

1. Cut out the motif with a 1/4" border.
2. Place motif in warm water for 30 seconds.
3. Remove from water and slide the image on the soap. While still wet, carefully adjust the decal and smooth out wrinkles and air bubbles with the tip of your finger. Let soap and decal dry before using.

You can make your own soap decals with image transfer paper. Simply color photocopy photographs or any other image on transfer paper, then follow the instructions above to adhere the image to the soap. An example is #297 Photo Soaps.

Laminated Soaps

Another technique for decorating a soap with an image is to laminate the design and place it on top of the soap before packaging. The laminated design can be taken off before the soap is used. Use this technique to decorate the soap for packaging (see #76 West Coast Native) or to save the image (see #298 Wedding Soap).

Combined Techniques

You can, of course, combine decorating and molding techniques for infinite design possibilities. For example, #96 Yin/Yang is a layered soap that is embossed with a soap stamp and dry brushed with gold paint. ❑

The Recipes

So here they are – the 300 recipes. Each one lists the supplies you need (soap bases, colorants, fragrances, additives, and molds, as well as other supplies) and references the technique used.

Many of the recipes can easily be doubled or tripled and can be made using the hand-milled soapmaking method. For instructions on the hand-milled method, see my books *Beautiful Handmade Natural Soaps* (Sterling, 1998) or *Melt & Pour Soapmaking* (Sterling, 2000), which includes a section on hand-milling.

Avoiding Confusion About Soapmaking Terms in Recipes

Some terms can be confusing and need a bit of explanation:

Coconut oil is a soap base, a fragrance oil, and an additive. When I refer to the soap base, it is listed in the recipe as "coconut oil soap base." References to coconut fragrance oil are listed under "Fragrance." When I refer to coconut oil – an unscented, white oil that is semi-solid at room temperature and used to add moisturizing qualities to the soap – it is listed as an "Additive."

Aloe vera is both an additive and a fragrance oil. Aloe vera gel, which may be added to melted soap base for its healing qualities, is listed under "Additives." Aloe vera fragrance is listed under "Fragrance."

Cocoa butter can be an additive and a fragrance oil. Cocoa butter – the additive – is an unscented, light amber oil that is solid at room temperature. When added to soap base, it makes the resulting soap harder and extra emollient. Cocoa butter fragrance is listed under "Fragrance."

When an ingredient is listed as a "Fragrance," it is the *name of a fragrance oil,* not the actual item. Examples include fragrances such as brown sugar, bubblegum, candy cane, earth, cucumber, and butter cream, to name a few.

When an ingredient is listed under "Colorants," it is the *name of a colorant,* not the actual item. This includes color names such as "sand" and "coffee." If actual ground coffee, for example, were added for color, it would be listed as an "Additive," not a "Colorant."

TIPS

Important points to remember:

• The amount of melted soap base in each recipe is shown in liquid ounces.

• For many recipes, you can substitute a different soap base. For example, a clear glycerin soap base can be substituted for a glycerin soap base with added olive oil.

• White coconut oil soap base is a very different soap from glycerin soap base – the two should **not** be mixed together. However, all glycerin soaps can be mixed without harming the qualities of the finished soap bar.

24

Natural Additives in Soaps

11

Adding natural additives to melt and pour soap bases is the focus in this first section of recipes. Some soaps do not contain colorant, as the additives give the bars distinct, natural tones. The additives give nourishing, gentle scrubbing, moisturizing, and other beneficial qualities to your finished soaps. Remember to keep to the amounts listed; too much can make your bars soft and messy. ❑

Recipe 1
Chamomile Oatmeal

Makes two 4-oz. bars.

Melt & Pour Base: 8 oz. coconut oil soap base

Fragrance: 10 drops chamomile

Colorant: 5 drops yellow

Additives: 1 teaspoon dried chamomile flowers, 1/2 teaspoon whole oatmeal

Molds: 4-oz. rectangle

See the Basic Technique.

Recipe 2
Oatmeal Cinnamon

Makes two 4-oz. bars.

Melt & Pour Base: 8 oz. coconut oil soap base

Fragrance: 15 drops cinnamon

Colorant: 2 drops red

Additives: 1/4 teaspoon powdered cinnamon, 1/2 teaspoon toasted whole oatmeal mixed in 1 teaspoon liquid glycerin

Molds: 4-oz. dome

See the Basic Technique.

Recipe 3
Cinnamon Rosemary Scrub

Makes two 3-oz. bars.

Melt & Pour Base: 6 oz. coconut oil soap base

Fragrance: 10 drops cinnamon, 5 drops rosemary

Colorant: 3 drops green

Additives: 1/4 teaspoon cornmeal, 1/4 teaspoon cinnamon, and 1/4 teaspoon dried whole rosemary mixed in 1 teaspoon glycerin

Molds: 3-oz. oval

See the Basic Technique.

Recipe 4
Cranberry Cornmeal

Makes two 4-oz. slices.

Melt & Pour Base: 8 oz. clear glycerin soap base

Fragrance: 10 drops cranberry

Additives: 1/4 teaspoon cornmeal, 1/2 teaspoon dried cranberry, chopped fine, 6 drops grapefruit seed extract

Molds: 2-1/2" round plastic tube mold

See "Tube Molded Soaps" in the Designer Techniques section.

Recipe 5
Nutty Oatmeal

(not pictured)

Makes two 4-oz. bars.

Melt & Pour Base: 8 oz. coconut oil soap base

Fragrance: 20 drops Almond milk, 10 drops coconut

Additives: 1/2 teaspoon toasted oatmeal, 1/2 teaspoon toasted coconut

Molds: 4-oz. dome

See the Basic Technique.

Recipe 6
Fruity Oatmeal

(not pictured)

Makes two 4-oz. slices.

Melt & Pour Base: 8 oz. clear glycerin soap base

Fragrance: 10 drops blackberry, 10 drops apricot

Additives: 1/2 teaspoon oatmeal

Molds: 2-1/2" round plastic tube mold

See "Tube Molded Soaps" in the Designer Techniques section.

Recipe 7
Cinnamon Comfort

(not pictured)

Makes two 4-oz. bars.

Melt & Pour Base: 8 oz. coconut oil soap base

Fragrance: 10 drops cinnamon, 10 drops pear, and 10 drops vanilla

Colorant: 4 drops red, 2 drops black for a tan hue

Additives: 1/4 teaspoon powdered cinnamon, seeds scraped from a 2" piece of vanilla bean and mixed with 1 teaspoon of liquid glycerin.

Molds: 4-oz. dome

See the Basic Technique.

Recipe 8
Chocolate Chip Cookie Soap

(not pictured)

Makes two 4-oz. bars.

Melt & Pour Base: 8 oz. whitened glycerin soap base

Fragrance: 10 drops cinnamon, 20 drops brown sugar and 10 drops chocolate

Colorant: pinch of cocoa powder mixed in 1-teaspoon liquid glycerin for a soft tan hue

Additives: 2 teaspoons cocoa butter

Molds: 3" round plastic tube mold

See "Tube Molded Soaps" and "Chunk Style Soaps" in the Designer Techniques section.

Recipe 9
Apple Cinnamon

Makes two 3-oz. bars.

Melt & Pour Base: 6 oz. coconut oil soap base

Fragrance: 15 drops spicy apple

Colorant: Pinch of paprika

Additives: 1/4 teaspoon powdered cinnamon mixed in 1 teaspoon liquid glycerin

Molds: 3-oz. rectangle

See the Basic Technique.

Recipe 10
Cinnamon Orange

Makes two 2.5-oz. bars.

Melt & Pour Base: 5 oz. clear glycerin soap base

Fragrance: 5 drops cinnamon, 10 drops orange

Colorant: Pinch of turmeric

Additives: 1/4 teaspoon cinnamon and 1/4 teaspoon orange granules mixed in 1 teaspoon liquid glycerin

Molds: 2.5-oz. round

See the Basic Technique.

Recipe 11
Cinnamon Spice

Makes two heart-shaped bars.

Melt & Pour Base: 5 oz. clear glycerin soap base

Fragrance: 10 drops mixed spice

Colorant: 4 drops red

Additives: 1/4 teaspoon cinnamon, 1/8 teaspoon clove, and 1/4 teaspoon poppy seeds mixed in 1 teaspoon liquid glycerin

Molds: 3-oz. heart, 2-oz. heart

See the Basic Technique.

Recipe 12
Chamomile Cinnamon

Makes two 4-oz. bars.

Melt & Pour Base: 8 oz. whitened glycerin soap base

Fragrance: 15 drops chamomile, 5 drops cinnamon

Additives: 1/4 teaspoon cinnamon and 1/4 teaspoon dried chamomile flowers mixed in 1 teaspoon liquid glycerin

Molds: 4-oz. rectangle

Other Supplies: Soap decal of girl with flowers

See "Soaps with Decals" in the Designer Techniques section.

Recipe 13
Honey Bee

Makes two bee-shaped bars.

Melt & Pour Base: 8.5 oz. clear glycerin soap base

Fragrance: 15 drops honey

Colorant: 4 drops orange, 1 drop blue (to make an amber color)

Additives: 1/2 teaspoon bee pollen, 1 teaspoon honey

Molds: 4.25-oz. bee mold

See the Basic Technique.

Recipe 14
Almond Honey

Makes two 2-oz. bars.

Melt & Pour Base: 4 oz. coconut oil soap base

Fragrance: 10 drops almond, 10 drops chamomile, 8 drops honey

Colorant: 1 drop blue, 3 drops orange (to make a soft amber hue)

Additives: 1/2 teaspoon ground almond

Molds: 2-oz. honeycomb and bee mold

See the Basic Technique.

13

Recipe 15
Honey Cream

Makes two 2-oz. bars.

Melt & Pour Base: 4 oz. glycerin soap base with added goat's milk

Fragrance: 10 drops vanilla cream, 5 drops honey

Additives: 1 teaspoon honey and seeds from a 1" piece vanilla bean

Molds: 2-oz. hexagon

See the Basic Technique. To remove the seeds from a vanilla bean pod, cut it open and scrape out the tiny, fragrant black seeds.

Recipe 16
Honey Blossom

Makes three bars, 1" thick

Melt & Pour Base: 8 oz. whitened glycerin soap base with added coconut oil

Fragrance: 5 drops coconut, 10 drops honey

Additives: 2 teaspoons dried calendula petals

Molds: Plastic tube mold, 3" flower

See "Tube Molded Soaps" in the Designer Techniques section.

Recipe 17
Fruited Honey

(not pictured)

Makes two bee-shaped bars.

Melt & Pour Base: 8.5 oz. clear glycerin soap base

Fragrance: 10 drops papaya, 10 drops apricot, 5 drops honey

Colorant: 4 drops yellow

Additives: 1 teaspoon honey, 1-teaspoon sweet almond oil

Molds: 4.25-oz. bee mold

See the Basic Technique.

Recipe 18
Honey Bear

(not pictured)

Melt & Pour Base: 8 oz whitened glycerin soap base

Fragrance: 5 drops honey, 10 drops butter cream and 10 drops pear

Colorant: 5 drops orange and two drops blue for an amber hue

Molds: 4-ounce teddy bear mold

See the Basic Technique.

Recipe 19
Chocolate Mint

(not pictured)

Melt & Pour Base: 8 oz. coconut oil soap base

Fragrance: 10 drops chocolate mint, 10 drops coconut

Colorant: pinch of cocoa powder

Additives: 2 teaspoons cocoa butter

Molds: 4-oz. dome

See the Basic Technique.

Recipe 20
Refresh-mint

(not pictured)

Makes two 4-oz. slices.

Melt & Pour Base: 8 oz. clear glycerin soap base

Fragrance: 5 drops green apple, 5 drops lime, 10 drops spearmint

Colorant: 5 drops green

Additives: 1-teaspoon liquid glycerin

Molds: 2-1/2" round plastic tube mold

See "Tube Molded Soaps" in the Designer Techniques section.

Recipe 21
Mango Mint

Makes two 2.5-oz. bars.

Melt & Pour Base: 5 oz. glycerin soap base with added hemp Oil

Fragrance: 15 drops mango, 5 drops peppermint

Additives: 1/2 teaspoon dried peppermint

Molds: 2.5-oz. round mold

See the Basic Technique.

Recipe 22
Cucumber Mint

Makes two 1" bars.

Melt & Pour Base: 3 oz. whitened glycerin soap base, 3 oz. clear glycerin soap base

Fragrance: 20 drops cucumber, 10 drops peppermint

Colorant: 4 drops green

Molds: 2" round tube mold, 2.75" round tube mold

Other Supplies: 3 plastic straws

See "Tube Molded Soaps" in the Designer Techniques section and follow these instructions:

1. Press 3 plastic straws between your thumb and index finger to form them into flattened ovals. Press the straws into the base of a prepared 2" round mold.
2. Melt 3 oz. whitened glycerin soap base. Add 20 drops cucumber fragrance and pour soap into the 2" round mold around the straws. Let set and release soap.
3. Place the white column of soap into the 2.75" round prepared mold. Melt 3 oz. clear glycerin soap base. Add 10 drops peppermint fragrance oil and 4 drops green colorant.
4. Remove the straws. Pour the melted clear green glycerin soap around the edge and in the holes created by the straws. Let soap set.
5. Release, trim, and slice into two 1" bars.

Recipe 23
Aloe Vera Mint

Makes two 3-oz. bars.

Melt & Pour Base: 6 oz. aquamarine-colored glycerin soap base

Fragrance: 20 drops herbal mint

Additives: 1 teaspoon aloe vera gel, 1/2 teaspoon dried peppermint leaves

Molds: 3-oz. oval

See the Basic Technique.

Recipe 24
Spearmint Sage Stars

Makes three star-shaped bars.

Melt & Pour Base: 6 oz. opaque sage-colored glycerin soap base

Fragrance: 10 drops spearmint, 5 drops sage

Additives: 1 teaspoon dried sage

Molds: 1-oz. star, 2-oz. star, 3-oz. star

See the Basic Technique.

Recipe 25
Oriental Rose

Makes two 2-oz. bars.

Melt & Pour Base: 4 oz. glycerin soap base with added goat's milk

Fragrance: 10 drops spice blend, 10 drops rose

Additives: 1/4 teaspoon *each* of ginseng powder, ginger, and cinnamon mixed in 1 teaspoon liquid glycerin

Molds: 2-oz. round

See the Basic Technique.

Recipe 26
Spice Rose

Makes two 3-oz. heart-shaped bars.

Melt & Pour Base: 6 oz. rose quartz-colored glycerin soap base

Fragrance: 15 drops rose petals, 5 drops clove

Additives: 1/4 teaspoon powdered ginger and 1/4 teaspoon powdered cloves mixed in 1 teaspoon liquid glycerin

Molds: 3-oz. embossed heart

See the Basic Technique.

Recipe 27
Rosie O'Bar

Makes two rose-shaped bars.

Melt & Pour Base: 5 oz. coconut oil soap base

Fragrance: 20 drops Victorian rose

Colorant: 5 drops red

Additives: 1/4 teaspoon paprika

Molds: 2.5-oz. rose mold

See the Basic Technique.

Recipe 28
Amber Rose

Makes two 1" oval slices.

Melt & Pour Base: 10 oz. clear glycerin soap base

Fragrance: 10 drops amber romance, 10 drops Victorian rose

Colorant: 6 drops white, 2 drops red, 2 drops green

Additives: 1 teaspoon dried rose petals

Molds: 1.5" blossom tube mold, 1.5" heart tube mold, 3" oval tube mold

See "Tube Molded Soaps" in the Designer Techniques section and follow these instructions:

1. Melt 2 oz. clear glycerin soap base, add 3 drops white colorant and 2 drops red colorant. Pour soap into a prepared 1.5" blossom tube mold. Let set and release soap.
2. Pour 2 oz. clear glycerin soap base with 3 drops white colorant and 2 drops green colorant into a prepared 1.5" heart tube mold. Let set and release soap.
3. Place the pink blossom soap column in a prepared 3" oval tube mold. Cut the green heart soap column in half to create the leaves. Place in the oval column around the blossom. Cool in

refrigerator.

4. Melt 6 oz. clear glycerin soap base. Add 10 drops amber romance fragrance, 10 drops Victorian rose fragrance, and 1 teaspoon dried rose petals. Pour into the oval mold around the cooled soap columns. Let soap set, release, trim, and slice into two 1" slices.

Recipe 29
English Rose

(not pictured)

Make two 4-oz. bars.

Melt & Pour Base: 8 oz. whitened glycerin soap base with added goat's milk

Fragrance: 20 drops English rose, 10 drops romance

Colorant: 4 drops red

Additives: 1 teaspoon dried pink rose petals, pinch iridescent powder

Molds: 4-oz. dome

See the Basic Technique.

Recipe 30
Rose Musk

(not pictured)

Makes two 4-oz. bars.

Melt & Pour Base: 8 oz. coconut oil soap base

Fragrance: 20 drops Victorian rose, 10 drops musk, 10 drops very vanilla

Colorant: 4 drops red, 1 drop green for a dusty rose hue

Additives: seeds scraped from a 1" piece vanilla bean mixed with 1-teaspoon liquid glycerin

Molds: 4-oz. rectangle

See the Basic Technique.

27

25

36

33

27

41

Recipe 31
Pear Spice

(not pictured)

Makes two 4-oz. bars.

Melt & Pour Base: 8 oz. coconut oil soap base

Fragrance: 20 drops brandied pear, 10 drops spice blend, 10 drops vanilla

Additives: 1/4 teaspoon cinnamon powder, 1/4 teaspoon ground cloves mixed into 1 teaspoon liquid glycerin

Molds: 4-oz. rectangle

See the Basic Technique.

Recipe 32
Lavender Spice

(not pictured)

Makes two 4-oz. bars.

Melt & Pour Base: 8 oz. whitened glycerin soap base

Fragrance: 20 drops lavender, 10 drops spice blend

Colorant: 4 drops red, 2 drops blue for a soft lavender hue

Molds: 4-oz. rectangle

See the Basic Technique.

Sensational Scents

Much of the appeal of a soap often comes from the scent. The soaps in this section smell wonderful! The next four recipes are great scents for men.

Recipe 33
Almond Spice

Makes two 3-oz. bars.

Melt & Pour Base: 6 oz. coconut oil soap base

Fragrance: 10 drops honey almond, 5 drops clove, 5 drops cinnamon

Additives: 1 teaspoon ground almond, 1/2 teaspoon cinnamon powder mixed in 1 teaspoon liquid glycerin

Molds: 3-oz. oval

See the Basic Technique.

Recipe 34
Ginger Spice

Makes two bars.

Melt & Pour Base: 5 oz. clear glycerin soap base

Fragrance: 5 drops ginger, 5 drops clove, 10 drops cinnamon, 10 drops tangerine

Additives: 1/2 teaspoon powdered ginger mixed in 1 teaspoon liquid glycerin

Molds: 2.5-oz. fleur de lis

See the Basic Technique.

Recipe 35
Lime Spice

The edges are beveled with a soap beveller. This makes two bars.

Melt & Pour Base: 6 oz. clear glycerin soap base with added olive oil

Fragrance: 10 drops lime, 5 drops spice blend

Additives: 1/4 teaspoon cinnamon powder mixed in 1 teaspoon liquid glycerin

Molds: 3-oz. rectangle

See the Basic Technique.

Recipe 36
Musk Spice

Makes two 3-oz. bars.

Melt & Pour Base: 6 oz. whitened glycerin soap base

Fragrance: 10 drops bay rum, 5 drops clove, 8 drops musk

Colorant: 5 drops coffee

Additives: 1 teaspoon ground cloves mixed in 1 teaspoon liquid glycerin

Molds: 4-oz. dome, filled three-quarters full

See the Basic Technique.

Recipe 37
Hazelnut Vanilla

Makes two 3-oz. bars.

Melt & Pour Base: 6 oz. coconut oil soap base

Fragrance: 5 drops hazelnut, 10 drops vanilla

Additives: Seeds from a 1" piece vanilla bean, 1 teaspoon ground hazelnuts, 5 drops grapefruit seed extract

Molds: 3-oz. round

See the Basic Technique. To remove the seeds from a vanilla bean pod, cut it open and scrape out the tiny, fragrant black seeds.

Recipe 38
Vanilla Almond

Makes two bars.

Melt & Pour Base: 7 oz. whitened glycerin soap base with added coconut oil

Fragrance: 8 drops almond milk, 8 drops vanilla

Molds: 3-oz. and 4-oz. embossed rectangle molds

See the Basic Technique.

Recipe 39
Vanilla Cream

Makes two small bars.

Melt & Pour Base: 3 oz. whitened glycerin soap base with added coconut oil

Fragrance: 10 drops vanilla cream

Additives: 1/2 teaspoon powdered whole milk and seeds from a 1/2" piece of vanilla bean mixed in 1 teaspoon liquid glycerin

Molds: 1-oz. and 2-oz. fancy soap rectangles

See the Basic Technique. To remove the seeds from a vanilla bean pod, cut it open and scrape out the tiny, fragrant black seeds.

43

57

44

51

Recipe 40
Vanilla Spice

(not pictured)

Makes two 4-oz. bars.

Melt & Pour Base: 8 oz. clear glycerin soap base with added olive oil

Fragrance: 20 drops vanilla

Additives: 1/4 teaspoon cinnamon powder, 1/4 teaspoon ginger powder, 1/4 teaspoon clove powder mixed into 1-teaspoon liquid glycerin

Molds: 4-oz. dome, filled three-quarters full

See the Basic Technique.

Recipe 41
Lavender Vanilla

(not pictured)

Makes two 4-oz. bars.

Melt & Pour Base: 8 oz. coconut oil soap base

Fragrance: 10 drops lavender, 10 drops vanilla, 5 drops jasmine

Additives: 1 Vitamin E capsule, 1-teaspoon liquid glycerine, 1/8 teaspoon iridescent powder

Molds: 4-oz. dome, filled three-quarters full

See the Basic Technique.

Recipe 42
Candy Rose

Makes four tiny (1/2 oz.) bars.

Melt & Pour Base: 2 oz. whitened glycerin soap base

Fragrance: 5 drops vanilla cream, 5 drops English rose

Colorant: 3 drops perfect pink

Additives: 1/8 teaspoon pearlescent powder

Molds: Small rose

See the Basic Technique.

Recipe 43
Raspberry Papaya

Makes two bars.

Melt & Pour Base: 3 oz. coral blush-colored opaque glycerin soap base

Fragrance: 10 drops *each* papaya and raspberry

Additives: 1/2 teaspoon paprika

Molds: 1-1/2-oz. shell

See the Basic Technique.

Recipe 44
Orange Sandalwood

The edges are beveled with a soap beveler. This makes two bars.

Melt & Pour Base: 6 oz. clear glycerin soap base

Fragrance: 10 drops sweet orange, 8 drops sandalwood

Colorant: 5 drops orange

Additives: 1/2 teaspoon rice bran

Molds: 3-oz. rectangle

See the Basic Technique.

Recipe 45
Tropical Floral

(not pictured)

Makes two 4-oz. bars.

Melt & Pour Base: 8 oz. coconut oil soap base

Fragrance: 10 drops mango, 15 drops sweet orange, 10 drops lavender

Additives: 1/2 teaspoon orange peel granules, 1/2 teaspoon finely shredded coconut

Molds: 4-oz. rectangle

See the Basic Technique.

Recipe 46
Fruit Blossom

(not pictured)

Makes two 4-oz. bars.

Melt & Pour Base: 8 oz. coconut oil soap base

Fragrance: 10 drops melon, 10 drops papaya and 15 drops jasmine

Colorant: 3 drops red

Additives: 1 teaspoon cocoa butter

Molds: 4-oz. dome

See the Basic Technique.

Recipe 47
Strawberry Mint

(not pictured)

Makes two 4-oz. bars.

Melt & Pour Base: 4 ounces whitened glycerin soap base, 4 ounces clear glycerin soap

Fragrance: 15 drops strawberry, 10 drops spearmint

Colorant: 2 drops red added to white soap, 3 drops green added to clear soap

Molds: 4-oz. rectangle

See "Marbled Soaps" in Designer Techniques section.

Recipe 48
Berry Blend

(not pictured)

Makes two 4-oz. bars.

Melt & Pour Base: 8 oz. whitened glycerin soap base with added goat's milk

Fragrance: 10 drops Almond milk, 10 drops vanilla, 10 drops strawberry and 10 drops raspberry

Colorant: 4 drops red

Molds: 4-oz. rectangle

See the Basic Technique.

52

53

54

42

47

Recipe 49
Green Tea Cardamom

(not pictured)

Makes one frog-shaped soap that looks like jade.

Melt & Pour Soap Base: 2 oz. coconut oil soap base, 2 oz. clear glycerin soap base

Fragrance: 20 drops green tea

Colorant: 6 drops green

Additives: 1/4 teaspoon ground cardamom, 1/2 teaspoon green tea

Molds: 3 oz. rectangle, 4 oz. rubber frog

See "Chunk Style Soaps" in the Designer Techniques section and follow these instructions:

1. Add 10 drops green tea fragrance, 3 drops green colorant, 1/4 teaspoon ground cardamom, and 1/2 teaspoon green tea to 2 oz. melted coconut oil soap base. Pour into a rectangle mold and let harden. Release and cut into small (1/2") cubes.

2. Place the soap cubes into a 4-oz. rubber frog mold. Add 10 drops green tea fragrance oil and 3 drops green colorant to 2 oz. melted clear glycerin soap. Pour into the frog mold. Release when completely cool.

Recipe 50
Orange Violet

Simple violets were painted on the finished bars with soap paint. This makes two bars.

Melt & Pour Base: 6 oz. whitened glycerin soap base

Fragrance: 10 drops sweet orange, 10 drops violet

Colorant: 3 drops orange

Additives: 1/2 teaspoon orange granules

Molds: 3-oz. oval

Other Supplies: Soap paint

See "Painted Soaps" in the Designer Techniques section.

Recipe 51
Sparkling Strawberry Watermelon

Makes one large bar or two slices.

Melt & Pour Base: 4 oz. clear glycerin soap base

Fragrance: 10 drops strawberry, 10 drops watermelon

Colorant: 3 drops red

Additives: Pinch of poppy seeds, 1/8 teaspoon iridescent powder

Molds: Round plastic tube mold, 2" diameter

See "Tube Molded Soaps" in the Designer Techniques section.

Recipe 52
Strawberry Mango Orange

Makes two bars.

Melt & Pour Base: 6.5 oz. coconut oil soap base

Fragrance: 10 drops strawberry, 10 drops mango, 5 drops sweet orange

Colorant: 2 drops red, 3 drops orange (to make a soft coral hue)

Additives: 1/4 teaspoon orange granules

Molds: 3.25-oz. radiant heart

See the Basic Technique.

Recipe 53
Cucumber Strawberry

Makes two bars.

Melt & Pour Base: 6 oz. coconut oil soap base

Fragrance: 10 drops cucumber, 8 drops strawberry

Colorant: 3 drops red, 1 drop black

Additives: 1/2 teaspoon dried strawberry leaf

Molds: 3-oz. rectangle

See the Basic Technique.

55

56

58

Recipe 54
Strawberry Cream

Makes five small bars.

Melt & Pour Base: 4 oz. whitened glycerin soap base with added goat's milk

Fragrance: 12 drops strawberry

Colorant: 1 drop red

Additives: 1/4 teaspoon powdered goat's milk mixed in 1 teaspoon liquid glycerin

Molds: 1-oz. and 1/2 oz. folk art motifs

See the Basic Technique.

Recipe 55
Lavender Lemon

Makes two bars.

Melt & Pour Base: 4 oz. clear glycerin soap base

Fragrance: 10 drops lavender, 10 drops lemon

Colorant: 4 drops green

Molds: 2-oz. fancy round

See the Basic Technique.

Recipe 56
Lemon Sage Scrub

Makes two bars.

Melt & Pour Base: 4 oz. coconut oil soap base

Fragrance: 5 drops sage, 10 drops lemon

Colorant: 3 drops yellow, 1 drop green

Additives: 1/2 teaspoon dried sage leaves, 1/2 teaspoon cornmeal mixed in 1 teaspoon liquid glycerin

Molds: 2-oz. round

See the Basic Technique.

Recipe 57
Lemongrass Lime

The square soap is cut in half diagonally to make two triangle-shaped bars. All edges are beveled with a soap beveller.

Melt & Pour Base: 5 oz. glycerin soap base with added olive oil

Fragrance: 10 drops lime, 10 drops lemongrass

Colorant: 3 drops green

Additives: 1/2 teaspoon dried lemongrass

Molds: 5-oz. square

See the Basic Technique.

Recipe 58
Summer Lemon

Makes two bars.

Melt & Pour Base: 3 oz. coconut oil soap base

Fragrance: 5 drops lemon, 5 drops peppermint

Colorant: 3 drops yellow, 1 drop green

Molds: 1.5-oz. lemon-shaped

See "Soaps with Defined Color Areas" in the Designer Techniques section.

Recipe 59
Citrus Dream

Makes two bars.

Melt & Pour Base: 8 oz. coconut oil soap base

Fragrance: 5 drops lemon, 5 drops lime, 5 drops pink grapefruit, 10 drops vanilla

Colorant: 4 drops orange

Molds: 4-oz. sun-shape

See the Basic Technique.

Recipe 60
Orange Hemp

Makes two bars.

Melt & Pour Base: 8 oz. glycerin soap base with added hemp oil

Fragrance: 10 drops sweet orange, 10 drops earth

Additives: 1/2 teaspoon dried eucalyptus leaves, crushed

Molds: 4-oz. rectangle

See the Basic Technique.

Recipe 61
Exotic Citrus

Makes two bars.

Melt & Pour Base: 3 oz. clear glycerin soap base

Fragrance: 5 drops bergamot, 5 drops tangerine, 5 drops mandarin

Colorant: 5 drops orange, 3 drops blue (for a dark amber hue)

Additives: 1 teaspoon dried, crushed bergamot leaves

Molds: 1.5-oz. round guest bar with flourish

See the Basic Technique.

Recipe 62
Mandarin Spice

The raised areas on the finished bars are accented with gold luster powder. This makes three bars.

Melt & Pour Base: 4 oz. whitened glycerin soap base

Fragrance: 10 drops mandarin, 8 drops spice blend

Colorant: 5 drops orange

Additives: 1/2 teaspoon powdered cloves mixed in 1 teaspoon liquid glycerin

Molds: 1.5-oz. rectangle guest bar with flourish

Other Supplies: Gold luster powder

See the Basic Technique.

Recipe 63
Orange Blossom

(not pictured)

Makes two 4-oz bars.

Melt & Pour Base: 8 oz. clear glycerin soap base

Fragrance: 20 drops sweet orange, 10 drops watermelon and 10 drops ylang-ylang

Colorant: 4 drops orange, 3 drops white for a translucent soft orange hue

Additives: pinch of gold glitter powder

Molds: 4 oz. rectangle

See the Basic Technique.

Recipe 64
Enthusiastic Orange

(not pictured)

Make two bars.

Melt & Pour Base: 8 oz. clear glycerin soap base with added hemp oil

Fragrance: 20 drops sweet orange, 10 drops tangerine, 10 drops neroli

Colorant: pinch Tumeric powder

Additives: pinch gold glitter powder

Molds: any 4 oz. size mold.

See the Basic Technique.

62

68

66

59

Healing Soap

These next four recipes are healing soaps. The additives and oils selected are all good for dry, itchy skin and help heal and disinfect scratched or damaged skin.

Recipe 65
Witch Hazel Anise

Makes two bars.

Melt & Pour Base: 5 oz. glycerin soap base with added hemp oil

Fragrance: 10 drops aniseed

Additives: 1 teaspoon witch hazel extract, 1 teaspoon witch hazel leaves

Molds: 2.5-oz. round

Other Supplies: Whole star anise, to accent the finished bar

See "Soaps with Decorative Accents" in the Designer Techniques section."

Recipe 66
Chicken Pox Soap

This is a recipe from my sister Lisa Simpson. She made it when her children were suffering from chicken pox to help relieve the itchiness. This makes two bars.

Melt & Pour Base: 4 oz. coconut oil soap base

Fragrance: 5 drops tea tree, 10 drops evening of primrose

Colorant: 3 drops red

Additives: 2 capsules vitamin E, 1/2 teaspoon ground oatmeal, 1 teaspoon aloe vera gel

Molds: 2-oz. lion

See the Basic Technique.

Recipe 67
Honeyed Tea Tree

Makes two bars.

Melt & Pour Base: 3 oz. glycerin soap base with added olive oil

Fragrance: 4 drops tea tree, 6 drops honey

Additives: 1 teaspoon honey

Molds: 1.5-oz. rectangle with leaf motif

See the Basic Technique.

Recipe 68
Eucalyptus and Rose Hip

Makes two bars.

Melt & Pour Base: 6 oz. coconut oil soap base

Fragrance: 20 drops eucalyptus therapy

Colorant: 3 drops China rose

Additives: 1 teaspoon rosehip powder mixed in 1 teaspoon liquid glycerin

Molds: 3.75-oz. deep rose, poured three-quarters full

See the Basic Technique.

Historical Soap

The next section of recipes takes you through the history of soap. We can only imagine when the first discovery of soap was made – it appears to have been available as early as 2000 B.C. At that time, it was used as a wound dressing; its cleansing properties had not yet been discovered.

Recipe 69
Fish Fossil

A plastic toy fish placed on the bottom of the mold creates the fossil. Makes one bar.

Melt & Pour Base: 3 oz. coconut oil

Fragrance: 10 drops amber

Colorant: 5 drops coffee

Additives: 1 teaspoon wheat germ and 1/2 teaspoon cinnamon mixed in 1 teaspoon liquid glycerin

Molds: 3-oz. rectangle mold lined with aluminum foil

Other Supplies: Plastic toy fish, aluminum foil

See "Fossil Soaps" in the Designer Techniques section.

Recipe 70
Centipede Fossil

A plastic toy centipede placed on the bottom of the mold creates the fossil. Makes one bar.

Melt & Pour Base: 5 oz. coconut oil soap base

Fragrance: 10 drops chocolate

Colorant: 5 drops sand

Additives: 1 teaspoon poppy seeds

Molds: 5-oz. square mold lined with aluminum foil

Other Supplies: Plastic toy centipede, aluminum foil

See "Fossil Soaps" in the Designer Techniques section.

Recipe 71
Beetle Fossil

A plastic toy beetle placed on the bottom of the mold creates the fossil. Makes one bar.

Melt & Pour Base: 4 oz. coconut oil soap base

Fragrance: 10 drops cocoa butter

Colorant: 4 drops black

Additives: 1/2 teaspoon poppy seed

Molds: 4-oz. rectangle mold lined with aluminum foil

Other Supplies: Plastic toy beetle, aluminum foil

See "Fossil Soaps" in the Designer Techniques section.

60

61

67

65

61

69

72

70

71

Recipe 72
Stone Age Ritual

Makes one bar.

Melt & Pour Base: 4 oz. coconut oil soap base

Fragrance: 10 drops earth

Colorant: 5 drops sand

Additives: 1/2 teaspoon dried bergamot leaves

Molds: 4-oz. rectangle lined with aluminum foil

Other Supplies: Stencil with prehistoric people motifs, soap paint

See "Painted Soaps" in the Designer Techniques section.

Recipe 73
Australian Spirit

Makes 2 irregular-shaped bars.

Melt & Pour Base: 8 oz. clear glycerin soap base

Fragrance: 10 drops eucalyptus, 5 drops jasmine, 5 drops mango

Colorant: 5 drops black

Molds: 5-oz. square lined with aluminum foil

Other Supplies: Stencil with jumping kangaroo motif, soap paint

See "Painted Soaps" in the Designer Techniques section.

Recipe 74
Fiji Tapa

This recipe is courtesy Environmental Technologies. It makes two bars.

Melt & Pour Base: 10 oz. whitened glycerin soap base

Fragrance: 10 drops coconut, 10 drops mango

Colorant: 5 drops red, 3 drops blue (for a purple hue)

Molds: 5-oz. square

Other Supplies: Stencil with decorative edges motif, soap paint

See "Painted Soaps" (Dip-Dot Painting, Stenciling) in the Designer Techniques section.

Recipe 75
Venus of Willendorf

Makes two bars.

Melt & Pour Base: 6.5 oz. whitened glycerin soap base

Fragrance: 20 drops bayberry spice

Colorant: 5 drops coffee

Additives: 1 teaspoon wheat bran

Molds: 3.25 oz. Venus of Willendorf

See the Basic Technique.

Recipe 76
West Coast Native

Makes two bars.

Melt & Pour Base: 3 oz. whitened glycerin and 3 oz. clear glycerin soap base

Fragrance: 15 drops cedarwood

Colorant: 4 drops sand (add to clear glycerin soap base), 4 drops coffee (add to white glycerin soap base)

Molds: 2.5 oz. round

Other Supplies: West Coast motif stamped and colored on white paper to use as a decoupage motif

See "Marbled Soaps" and "Decoupaged Soaps" in the Designer Techniques section.

Egyptian Influence

Egyptian bath rituals were well-chronicled but absent of soap. Instead, they used milks, essential oils, and white sand as an abrasive agent for cleaning.

81

79

79

77

81

Recipe 77
Cleopatra

Fine sea salt was used instead of sand for this body-polishing soap. Makes two bars.

Melt & Pour Base: 8.5 oz. coconut oil soap base

Fragrance: 10 drops frankincense, 15 drops jasmine

Additives: 2 teaspoons fine sea salt, 1/2 teaspoon iridescent powder, 1 tablespoon shea nut butter

Molds: 4.25-oz. arabesque oval

See the Basic Technique.

Recipe 78
Egyptian Pyramid

Makes one bar.

Melt & Pour Base: 3 oz. clear glycerin soap base

Fragrance: 20 drops milk 'n honey

Additives: 1/4 teaspoon gold luster powder added to clear glycerin soap base, 1/4 cup white soap base, cut into cubes

Molds: 4-oz. pyramid mold

See "Chunk Style Soaps" in the Designer Techniques section.

Recipe 79
Egyptian Musk

The edges are beveled with a soap beveler. This recipe makes two bars.

Melt & Pour Base: 7 oz. Wedgewood blue opaque glycerin soap base

Fragrance: 20 drops blue musk

Molds: 3-oz. and 4-oz. rectangles

Other Supplies: Stencil with Egyptian motifs, soap paint

See "Painted Soaps" in the Designer Techniques section.

Recipe 80
Ancient Shard

Makes one bar.

Melt & Pour Base: 3 oz. yellow opaque glycerin soap base

Fragrance: 10 drops mulberry, 10 drops musk

Additives: 1/4 cup white soap base, cut into cubes

Other Supplies: Gold Egyptian motif tissue paper

Molds: Aluminum foil formed into an irregular shape in the bottom of a plastic container

See "Chunk Style Soaps" and "Decoupaged Soaps" in the Designer Techniques section.

Roman Influence

The use of soap was not widespread in the Roman Empire but the cleansing properties of soap were known. Bathers at the grand Roman baths used oils in their cleansing rituals. The Arabs and later the Turks recognized the value of soap. When the Turks invaded the Byzantine Empire, soap was introduced to Europe on a grand scale.

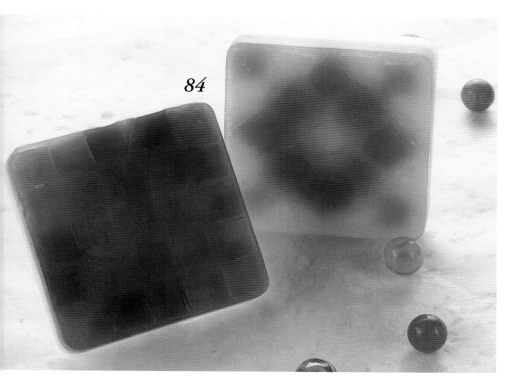

84

Recipe 81
Aegean

Makes two bars.

Melt & Pour Base: 2 oz. clear teal glycerin soap base, 1 oz. blue opaque glycerin soap base

Fragrance: 10 drops ocean breeze

Additives: 1/8 teaspoon iridescent powder added to blue opaque soap base

Molds: 1.5-oz. twin-fish guest mold

See "Soaps with Defined Color Areas" (pour-and-scrape) in the Designer Techniques section.

Recipe 82
Aphrodite

Makes one large bar (or two smaller bars if cut in half).

Melt & Pour Base: 3 oz. glycerin soap base with added coconut oil

Fragrance: 10 drops neroli, 5 drops lavender

Colorant: 3 drops sand (for a light cream hue)

Additives: 1/8-teaspoon gold luster powder

Molds: Venus de Milo rubber mold

See Basic Technique.

Recipe 83
Roman Bath

Makes two bars.

Melt & Pour Base: 1 oz. clear glycerin soap base, 5 oz. whitened glycerin soap base

Fragrance: 10 drops lavender, 5 drops bergamot

Additives: Pinch of gold luster powder to clear glycerin soap base

Molds: 3 oz. fancy heart

See "Soaps with Defined Color Areas" (pour-and-scrape) in the Designer Techniques section.

Recipe 84
Byzantine Mosaic

Makes two bars.

Melt & Pour Base: 2 oz. clear glycerin, 2 oz. whitened glycerin soap base

Fragrance: 5 drops patchouli, 10 drops pear

Additives: 1/4 cup colored soap cubes

Molds: 5-oz. square

See "Chunk Style Soaps" in the Designer Techniques section. Pour the clear glycerin in the mold, then arrange the colored cubes in a pattern. When set, pour in the white soap base.

80

78

82

83

Old World Soaps

It was not until the 13th century that soapmaking became established in Europe. Marseilles emerged as the first great center of soapmaking during the Middle Ages. Genoa and Venice in Italy and Castile in Spain became important centers through the 17th century, thanks to their plentiful supplies of olive oil. Though the Romans are credited with the discovery of soap, it is known that isolated tribes of Vikings and Celts discovered soap independently and are believed to have introduced soap to England around 1000 A.D.

Renaissance

Makes two bars.

Melt & Pour Base: 3 oz. glycerin soap base with added olive oil

Fragrance: 10 drops ylang-ylang

Colorant: 1 drop China rose colorant added to 1 oz. of melted soap base

Additives: 1 teaspoon olive oil, 1/4 teaspoon citric acid added to 2 oz. of melted soap base

Molds: 1.5-oz. round guest with embossed motif

See "Soaps with Defined Color Areas" (pour-and-scrape) in the Designer Techniques section.

Recipe 86
Creation

Makes two bars.

Melt & Pour Base: 8 oz. coconut oil soap base

Fragrance: 15 drops brandied pear

Colorant: 5 drops red, 3 drops blue (for a purple hue)

Molds: 4-oz. rectangle

Other Supplies: Decoupage paper with Michelangelo's creation motif

See "Decoupaged Soaps" in the Designer Techniques section.

Recipe 87
Tuscany

Makes two bars.

Melt & Pour Base: 4 oz. coconut oil soap base

Fragrance: 10 drops cinnamon, 5 drops bergamot, 10 drops vanilla

Additives: 1/2 teaspoon cocoa powder, 1/2 teaspoon cinnamon, 1/4 teaspoon powdered cloves, 1 teaspoon cocoa butter

Molds: 2 oz. round flourish

See the Basic Technique.

Recipe 88
Raphael Angel

Makes two bars.

Melt & Pour Base: 4 oz. coconut oil soap base

Fragrance: 10 drops gardenia, 10 drops cocoa butter

Additives: 2 vitamin E capsules, 1 teaspoon shea butter

Molds: 2-oz. angel

Other Supplies: Green soap paint, 1 teaspoon soap medium, 1/2 teaspoon gold luster powder

See "Painted Soaps" in the Designer Techniques section and follow these instructions for decorating:
1. To create the verdigris effect, dry brush with green soap paint. Let dry.
2. Mix soap medium and gold luster powder and brush over soap.

Recipe 89
Celtic Heart Knot

Makes two bars.

Melt & Pour Base: 7 oz. clear glycerin soap base

Fragrance: 5 drops rosemary, 5 drops peppermint, 5 drops wintergreen

Colorant: 5 drops green

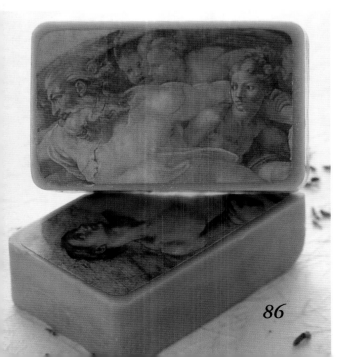

86

Additives: Pinch of white iridescent powder added to 1 oz. of melted soap base

Molds: 3.5 oz. Celtic heart

See "Soaps with Defined Color Areas" (pour-and-scrape) in the Designer Techniques section.

Recipe 90
Celtic

Makes two bars.

Melt & Pour Base: 6 oz. coconut oil soap base

Fragrance: 15 drops fresh rain

Colorant: 4 drops avocado rind green

Molds: 3-oz. oval

Other Supplies Rubber stamp with Celtic knot motifs

See "Embossed Soaps" in the Designer Techniques section.

Recipe 91
Celtic Desire

Makes two bars.

Melt & Pour Base: 7 oz. glycerin with added hemp oil

Fragrance: 20 drops herbal mint

Additives: 1/2 teaspoon dried peppermint leaves, pinch of gold powder added to 1 oz. melted soap base

Molds: 3.5 oz. Celtic square

See "Soaps with Defined Color Areas" (pour-and-scrape) in the Designer Techniques section.

Recipe 92
Viking Quest

Makes two bars.

Melt & Pour Base: 7 oz. whitened glycerin soap base

Fragrance: 15 drops apricot

Colorant: 2 drops green mixed in 1 oz. melted soap base, 2 drops green mixed in 6 oz. melted soap base

Additives: Gold glitter added to 1 oz. of melted soap base

Molds: 4-oz. and 3-oz.

rectangles with embossed motifs

See "Soaps with Defined Color Areas" (pour-and-scrape) in the Designer Techniques section.

Recipe 93
Green Tea

This recipe, created by Maria Nerius, is courtesy of Delta Technical Coatings. It makes two bars.

Melt & Pour Base: 6 oz. green opaque glycerin soap base

Fragrance: 15 drops fresh rain

Colorant: Pinch of gold luster powder added to 1 oz. melted soap base

Additives: 1 teaspoon jasmine green tea added to 5 oz. melted soap base

Molds: 3-oz. Asian symbols

See "Soaps with Defined Color Areas" (pour-and-scrape) in the Designer Techniques section.

Recipe 94
Jade Egg

Makes one jade egg.

Melt & Pour Base: 3 oz. glycerin soap base with added hemp oil

Fragrance: 8 drops lemongrass, 5 drops neroli

Colorant: 4 drops spinach

Molds: 3-oz. three-dimensional egg mold

See the Basic Technique.

Recipe 95
Oriental Zen

Makes two bars.

Melt & Pour Base: 4 oz. red clear colored glycerin soap base, 1 oz. clear glycerin soap base

Fragrance: 10 drops apple-pear, 5 drops ginger

Additives: Pinch of gold luster powder added to clear melted soap base

Molds: 1.5-oz. chrysanthemum guest mold

See "Soaps with Defined Color Areas" (pour-and-scrape) in the Designer Techniques section.

91

89

92

90

93

94

96

Recipe 96
Yin/Yang

Makes two bars.

Melt & Pour Base: 2 oz. clear glycerin soap base, 2 oz. whitened glycerin soap base

Fragrance: 15 drops China rain

Additives: 1/8 teaspoon gold luster powder added to melted clear glycerin soap base

Molds: 2.5 oz. round

Other Supplies: Soap stamp with turtle motif, green soap paint, gold soap paint

See "Layered Soaps," "Embossed Soaps," and "Painted Soaps" in the Designer Techniques section. Dry brush the soaps with green and gold paints.

Royal Soaps

Commercially produced triple-milled soaps from France are still considered the finest quality soaps available for their silky hardness, lasting fragrance, and excellent emollient characteristics. Many fragrant recipes from past centuries are as popular today as they once were with royalty.

Recipe 97
Queen Mary

Mary Queen of Scots was known for her flawless, creamy smooth skin. Makes two bars.

Melt & Pour Base: 2 oz. clear glycerin soap base, 7 oz. whitened glycerin soap base

Fragrance: 10 drops vanilla, 5 drops apricot, 5 drops gardenia

Colorant: 1 drop red added to 1 oz. clear melted soap base, 3 drops sand colorant to melted whitened glycerin soap base

Additives: Pinch of pearlescent powder to 1 oz. melted clear soap base, pinch of gold glitter to 1 oz. melted clear soap base

Molds: 4.5-oz. heart and crown mold

See "Soaps with Defined Color Areas" (pour-and-scrape) in the Designer Techniques section.

Recipe 98
King Louis

Makes two bars.

Melt & Pour Base: 1 oz. clear glycerin soap base, 6 oz. whitened glycerin soap base

Fragrance: 10 drops vanilla, 5 drops lavender, 5 drops spiced plum

Colorant: 2 drops blue added to melted clear soap base

Additives: Pinch of pearlescent powder to the melted clear soap base

Molds: 3.5-oz. radiant heart

See "Soaps with Defined Color Areas" (pour-and-scrape) in the Designer Techniques section.

Recipe 99
French Fields

Makes two bars.

Melt & Pour Base: 1 oz. clear glycerin soap base, 3 oz. whitened glycerin soap base

Fragrance: 10 drops lavender, 5 drops neroli, 5 drops tangerine

Colorant: 5 drops red, 2 drops blue

Molds: 2-oz. fleur de lis and fancy square flourish mold

See "Soaps with Defined Color Areas" (pour-and-scrape) in the Designer Techniques section. Add 5 drops red colorant and 2 drops blue colorant to each melted soap base.

Recipe 100
French Cameo

Makes two bars.

Melt & Pour Base: 4 oz. whitened glycerin

Fragrance: 8 drops fleur

Colorant: 3 drops blue, 1 drop orange to 2 oz. of the melted soap base (for a Wedgewood blue hue)

Molds: 2 oz. large cameo

See "Soaps with Defined Color Areas" (pour-and-scrape) in the Designer Techniques section.

Art Inspired Soaps

Inspiration for soaps can come from many sources. Modern masterpieces and modern scents inspire these works of art soaps.

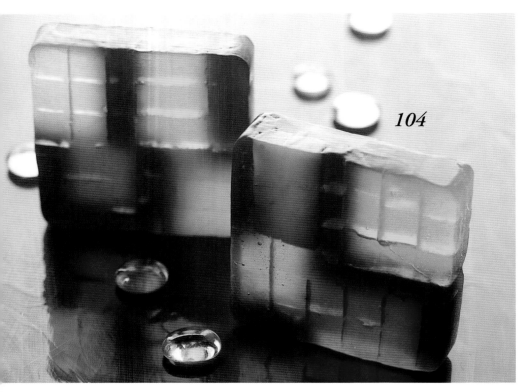

104

Recipe 103
Kiss

Inspired by Brancusi's "The Kiss," this makes two bars.

Melt & Pour Base: 8 oz. whitened glycerin soap base

Fragrance: 20 drops amber romance

Colorant: 5 drops red, 3 drops blue, 3 drops yellow (for a dusty purple hue)

Molds: 4-oz. rectangle

See "Carved Soaps" in the Designer Techniques section.

Recipe 104
Modern

Inspired by Piet Mondrian's "Composition with Red, Yellow and Blue," this makes one bar.

Melt & Pour Base: 4 oz. clear glycerin soap base

Fragrance: 5 drops blackberry, 5 drops very berry, 5 drops dewberry

Additives: White, yellow, red, dark purple, and blue soap cubes

Molds: 5-oz. square

See "Chunk Style Soaps" in the Designer Techniques section. Arrange the soap cubes carefully on the bottom of the mold and pour the clear melted base on top.

Recipe 101
Gauguin Tropical Rose

Makes two bars.

Melt & Pour Base: 10 oz. coconut oil soap base

Fragrance: 10 drops coconut, 10 drops rose petals

Colorant: 4 drops melon

Additives: 1 teaspoon coconut, 1/8 teaspoon iridescent powder

Molds: 5-oz. square

Other Supplies: Color photocopy of Paul Gauguin painting for decoupaging

See "Decoupaged Soaps" in the Designer Techniques section.

Recipe 102
Picasso

Makes two bars.

Melt & Pour Base: 6 oz. whitened glycerin soap base

Fragrance: 5 drops patchouli, 10 drops vanilla

Additives: Blue clear glycerin soap, pink clear glycerin soap, yellow soap cubes

Molds: 4-oz. rectangle

See "Chunk Style Soaps" in the Designer Techniques section. Using a soap beveler, make curls of blue soap. Cut triangles from the pink glycerin soap.

101

102

103

Painted Soaps

The next section is recipes for small decorative soaps that accent a larger bar. You can adhere the decorative soaps with clear melted soap or present them placed on top of the large bars, packaged together. The pairings provide a small fancy soap for the sink soap dish and a large bar for the shower or tub.

Recipe 106
Honeysuckle Blossom

This recipe is courtesy Environmental Technologies. It makes two bar sets.

Melt & Pour Base: 7 oz. whitened glycerin soap base

Fragrance: 10 drops honeysuckle

Colorant: 3 drops yellow to 2 oz. soap base (for blossoms)

Molds: 3 oz. round, small blossoms motif

See "Soaps with Decorative Accents" in the Designer Techniques section.

Recipe 107
Cherubs

Makes two bar sets.

Melt & Pour Base: 8 oz. whitened glycerin soap base

Fragrance: 10 drops baby powder, 5 drops lily of the valley

Colorant: 2 drops red, 1 drop blue to 2 oz. soap base (for cherubs), 3 drops red to 6 oz. soap base (for rectangle bar)

Additives: Pinch of iridescent powder (for cherubs)

Molds: Small cherub, 3 oz. rectangle

See "Soaps with Decorative Accents" in the Designer Techniques section.

Recipe 105
Raspberry Cream

This recipe is courtesy Environmental Technologies. It makes one bar set.

Melt & Pour Base: 5 oz. whitened glycerin soap base

Fragrance: 10 drops raspberry vanilla

Colorant: 1 drop red (for base of raspberry), 1 drop green (for raspberry leaves), 3 drops red (for oval bar)

Molds: 3 oz. oval, grape cluster (for the raspberry)

See "Soaps with Defined Color Areas" and "Soaps with Decorative Accents" in the Designer Techniques section.

107

108

106

105

Recipe 108
Fruit

Makes one bar set.

Melt & Pour Base: 2 oz. clear glycerin soap base (for fruit), 5 oz. whitened glycerin soap base (for square bar)

Fragrance: 5 drops mango, 10 drops melon

Colorant: Red (for strawberry), purple (for grapes), yellow (for banana), orange (for pear), 3 drops green (for the bar)

Molds: Tray of fruit motifs, 5-oz. square

Other Supplies: Green soap paint

See "Soaps with Decorative Accents" and "Painted Soaps" in the Designer Techniques section. Accent the fruit with a little green paint.

Recipe 109
Critters

Makes two bar sets.

Melt & Pour Base: 2 oz. clear glycerin soap base (for ladybugs), 4 oz. whitened glycerin soap base (for hexagon bar)

Fragrance: 10 drops blackberry

Colorant: 2 drops red (for ladybugs), 5 drops green (for bar)

Molds: Small ladybug, 2-oz. hexagon

Other Supplies: Black soap paint

See "Soaps with Decorative Accents" and "Painted Soaps" in the Designer Techniques section. Accent the ladybugs with a little black paint.

Recipe 110
Woodland

Makes two bar sets.

Melt & Pour Base: 4 oz. whitened glycerin

Fragrance: 6 drops brown sugar

Colorant: 3 drops sand (for acorns), 3 drops green (for leaves)

Additives: Pinch of powdered cinnamon (for acorns)

Molds: Woodland motifs tray

Other Supplies: Cream soap paint

See "Soaps with Decorative Accents" and "Painted Soaps" in the Designer Techniques section. Accent the acorns with a little cream paint.

Recipe 111
Festive

Makes one bar set.

Melt & Pour Base: 3 oz. whitened glycerin soap base (for Christmas motifs), 4 oz. clear glycerin soap base (for bar)

Fragrance: 10 drops eggnog, 5 drops candy cane

Colorant: 5 drops green (for the bar)

Molds: Christmas motifs tray, 3 oz. rectangle

Other Supplies: Green, red, and gold soap paint

See "Soaps with Decorative Accents" and "Painted Soaps" in the Designer Techniques section. Accent the Christmas motifs with red, green, and gold paint.

Recipe 112
Glitterflake

Makes two bar sets.

Melt & Pour Base: 4 oz. clear glycerin soap base

Fragrance: 10 drops vanilla, 10 drops violet

Colorant: 6 drops blue (for bar)

Additives: Pinch of iridescent powder (for snowflakes)

Molds: Snowflake motif tray, 2-oz. stars

See "Soaps with Decorative Accents" in the Designer Techniques section.

Recipe 113
Wild Rose

Makes two bar sets.

Melt & Pour Base: 5 oz. whitened glycerin soap base

Fragrance: 10 drops Victorian rose

Colorant: 1 drop red (for roses), 3 drops green (for bar)

Molds: Small rose motifs tray, 2-oz. round

See "Soaps with Decorative Accents" in the Designer Techniques section.

113

114

116

Recipe 114
Folk Art Heart

Makes two bar sets.

Melt & Pour Base: 5 oz. whitened glycerin soap base

Fragrance: 10 drops buttery maple

Colorant: 3 drops red (for hearts)

Molds: Folk art motifs tray, 2-oz. hearts

Other Supplies: White soap paint

See "Soaps with Decorative Accents" in the Designer Techniques section.

See "Soaps with Decorative Accents" and "Soap Painting" in the Designer Techniques section. Dry brush a little white paint over the folk art motifs.

Recipe 115
Sea Shells

Makes two bar sets.

Melt & Pour Base: 2 oz. whitened glycerin soap base (for shells), 4 oz. clear glycerin soap base (for rounds)

Fragrance: 10 drops Hawaiian rain

Colorant: Variety of blue, green, and white colors (for shells); 2 drops blue, 2 drops green (for bar)

Molds: Seashells motif tray, 2-oz. rounds

See "Soaps with Decorative Accents" in the Designer Techniques section.

Recipe 116
Cameo

Makes two bars.

Melt & Pour Base: 7 oz. whitened glycerin soap base

Fragrance: 5 drops jasmine, 5 drops coconut

Colorant: 2 drops blue, 1 drop orange (for a Wedgewood blue hue) (for cameo)

Additives: 1/2 teaspoon coconut (for bar)

Molds: Small cameo motif tray, 3-oz. oval

See "Soaps with Decorative Accents" and "Soaps with Defined Color Areas" (pour-and-scrape) in the Designer Techniques section.

Working Soaps

I like to call the soaps in this section "working soaps." They are formulated to scrub away dirt, smells, or harmful bacteria and to have extra special qualities for cleaning or soothing problem hands or surfaces

Recipe 117
Pumice Scrub

A cleansing soap with the polishing effects of pumice, it's great for feet and elbows. This makes one bar.

Melt & Pour Base: 4 oz. whitened glycerin soap base with added coconut oil

Fragrance: 10 drops peppermint

Additives: 1 teaspoon powdered pumice mixed in 1 teaspoon liquid glycerin

Molds: 4-oz. oval

See the Basic Technique.

Recipe 118
Oyster Shell

Ground oyster shell effectively exfoliates the skin and gives the soap a glistening appearance. This makes two bars.

Melt & Pour Base: 6 oz. clear glycerin soap base

Fragrance: 15 drops ocean breeze

Additives: 1 teaspoon powdered oyster shell, 1/8 teaspoon gold luster powder

Molds: 3-oz. clamshell

See the Basic Technique.

Recipe 119
Kitchen Soap

This great idea is courtesy of C. Kaila Westerman, author of Melt & Mold Soap Crafting *(Storey Book Publications). The embedded soap dish makes the soap self-draining and very practical for the kitchen. This makes two bars.*

Melt & Pour Base: 8 oz. clear glycerin soap base

Fragrance: 20 drops rosemary, 10 drops anise

Colorant: 5 drops green

Additives: 1/2 teaspoon coconut oil, 1/4 teaspoon sweet almond oil, 2 teaspoons French clay

Molds: 4-oz. rectangle

Other Supplies: Plastic soap saver

See "Embedded Soaps" in the Designer Techniques section.

115

117

118

Recipe 120
Dirt Buster

This soap bar is a gardener's best friend! The recipe is courtesy Environmental Technologies and makes two bars.

Melt & Pour Base: 6 oz. clear glycerin soap base

Fragrance: 6 drops lavender, 4 drops lime, 2 drops peppermint

Colorant: 5 drops red, 2 drops black (for a dark brown hue)

Additives: 1 teaspoon whole oatmeal, 1/2 teaspoon ground almonds, 1 teaspoon dried rosemary

Molds: 3-oz. rectangle

See the Basic Technique.

Recipe 121
Lemon Loofah Scrub

Makes two bars.

Melt & Pour Base: 4 oz. clear glycerin soap base

Fragrance: 10 drops lemon

Colorant: 4 drops yellow

Additives: 1 teaspoon small loofah pieces

Molds: 2-oz. lemon

See the Basic Technique.

Recipe 122
Kitchen Smell Dispel

The lemon and coffee scents help to remove strong odors such as onions and fish from your hands. This makes two bars.

Melt & Pour Base: 6 oz. clear glycerin soap base

Fragrance: 10 drops lemon, 10 drops espresso

Colorant: 4 drops red, 2 drops black (for dark brown hue)

Additives: 1 teaspoon freshly ground coffee, 1/2 teaspoon dried lemon granules

Molds: 3-oz. rectangle

See the Basic Technique.

Recipe 123
Antibacterial Soap

This is a strong disinfectant soap. The recipe makes two bars.

Melt & Pour Base: 6 oz. coconut oil soap base

Fragrance: 10 drops peppermint, 5 drops eucalyptus, 5 drops tea tree

Colorant: 5 drops green

Additives: 1 teaspoon dried eucalyptus, 1 teaspoon dried peppermint

Molds: 3-oz. oval

See the Basic Technique.

Recipe 124
Fisherman's Soap

The anise fragrance is said to disguise a human's smell when fishing. The small bars fit in a tackle box. This makes two bars.

Melt & Pour Base: 3 oz. whitened glycerin soap base

Fragrance: 15 drops aniseed

Additives: 1 teaspoon ground anise seeds

Molds: 1.5-oz. round with fish motif

See the Basic Technique.

119

121

123

120

122

124

Recipe 125
Tea Tree Tumble

This healing soap is for skin with scratches – great after a day of blackberry picking! This makes two bars.

Melt & Pour Base: 4 oz. coconut oil soap base

Fragrance: 10 drops tea tree

Colorant: 5 drops green

Additives: 1 teaspoon dried comfrey, 4 vitamin E capsules

Molds: 2 oz. round southwest motifs

See the Basic Technique.

Recipe 126
Shaving Soap

This recipe is courtesy Environmental Technologies.

Melt & Pour Base: 4 oz. coconut oil soap base

Fragrance: 10 drops peppermint, 10 drops cinnamon

Colorant: 5 drops orange

Additives: 1 teaspoon witch hazel, 3 vitamin E capsules, 1 teaspoon liquid glycerin

Molds: A shaving mug – the soap is poured right in!

See the Basic Technique.

Recipe 127
Sailor's Shaving Soap

This makes two bars.

Melt & Pour Base: 5 oz. coconut oil soap base

Fragrance: 20 drops bay rum

Colorant: 6 drops blue

Additives: 3 capsules vitamin E, 1 teaspoon aloe vera gel, 1 teaspoon coconut oil

Molds: 2.5-oz. round

See the Basic Technique.

Recipe 128
Ladies' Shaving Soap

Makes two bars.

Melt & Pour Base: 6 oz. coconut oil soap base

Fragrance: 10 drops milk 'n honey, 10 drops vanilla cream

Colorant: 5 drops red

Additives: 1 teaspoon cocoa butter, 1/2 teaspoon French clay, 3 vitamin E capsules, 8 drops grapefruit seed extract

Molds: 3 oz. embossed heart

See the Basic Technique.

Recipe 129
Soothing Hands

Makes two bars.

Melt & Pour Base: 4 oz. coconut oil soap base

Fragrance: 5 drops rosemary, 10 drops English rose

Colorant: 3 drops red, 4 drops yellow

Additives: 1 teaspoon ground oatmeal, 3 vitamin E capsules, 1/2 teaspoon ground rosemary, 1 teaspoon French clay

Molds: 2 oz. round with celestial motifs

See the Basic Technique.

Recipe 130
Artist's Brush Soap

This specialty soap is for cleaning artist's acrylic paint brushes – it really works well! Mold the soap in a can and use it only for brushes.

Melt & Pour Base: 4 oz. coconut oil soap base

Additives: 1 tablespoon fabric washing agent such as Woolite

Molds: 4-oz. tin

See the Basic Technique.

Recipe 131
Creative Hands

This gentle scrubbing soap is great for painters and rubber stampers! It makes two bars.

Melt & Pour Base: 4 oz. coconut oil soap base

Fragrance: 15 drops juniper therapy

Additives: 3 vitamin E capsules, 1 teaspoon coconut oil, 1 teaspoon liquid glycerin, 1 teaspoon French clay, 1 teaspoon ground pumice

Molds: 2-oz. round

Other Supplies: Soap stamp with pear motif

See "Stamped Soaps" in the Designer Techniques section.

Recipe 132
Hand Smoother

Here's another soap for working hands that need special care. the recipe makes two bars.

Melt & Pour Base: 7 oz. whitened glycerin soap base

Fragrance: 10 drops cucumber, 10 drops aniseed

Colorant: 3 drops green

Additives: 1 teaspoon pumice mixed in 1 teaspoon liquid glycerin

Molds: 3.25 Celtic heart

See the Basic Techniques.

126

129

127

128

130

132

131

125

Fruit Favorites

The following section features my favorite soaps. Bright and fun, they are surprisingly easy to make with tube molds.

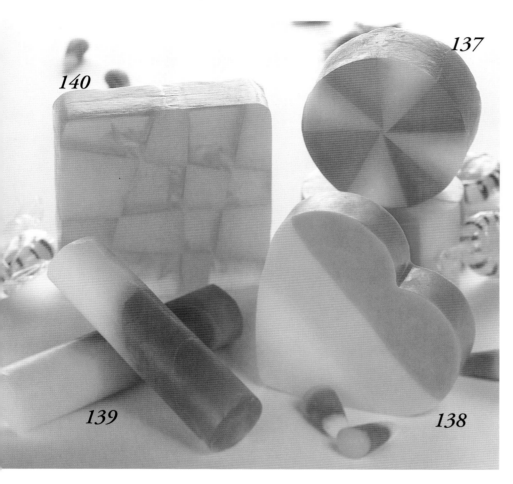

Recipe 133
Orange Slice

This recipe, courtesy Environmental Technologies, is available as a kit. It makes two bars, 3/4" thick.

Melt & Pour Base: 8 oz. clear glycerin soap base

Fragrance: 20 drops sweet orange

Colorant: 6 drops orange, 4 drops white

Molds: 2.5" tube, 3.25" tube

See "Tube Molded Soaps" in the Designer Techniques section and follow these instructions:

1. Melt 6 oz. of clear glycerin soap base. Add 20 drops sweet orange fragrance oil and 6 drops orange colorant. Pour into a prepared 2.5" tube mold. Set and release.
2. Cut orange soap column into six sections. Place in prepared 3.25" tube mold. Cool.
3. Melt 2 oz. of clear glycerin soap base. Add 4 drops white colorant. Pour in and around cooled sections. Set and release.
4. Trim ends and slice soap into two 3/4" thick bars.

Recipe 134
Lime Slice

Makes two bars, 3/4" thick.

Melt & Pour Base: 8 oz. clear glycerin soap base

Fragrance: 20 drops lime

Colorant: 6 drops green, 4 drops white

Molds: 2.5" tube, 3.25" tube

See "Tube Molded Soaps" in the Designer Techniques section and follow these instructions:

1. Melt 6 oz. of clear glycerin soap base. Add 20 drops lime fragrance oil and 6 drops green colorant. Pour into pre-pared 2.5" tube mold. Set and release.
2. Cut green soap column into six sections. Place in prepared 3.25" mold. Cool.
3. Melt 2 oz. of clear glycerin soap base. Add 4 drops white colorant. Pour in and around cooled sections. Set and release.
4. Trim ends and slice soap into two 3/4" thick bars.

Recipe 135
Lemon Slice

Makes two bars, 3/4" thick.

Melt & Pour Base: 8 oz. clear glycerin soap base

Fragrance: 20 drops lemon

Colorant: 8 drops yellow, 4 drops white

Molds: 2.5" tube, 3.25" tube

See "Tube Molded Soaps" in the Designer Techniques section and follow these instructions:

1. Melt 6 oz. of clear glycerin soap base. Add 20 drops lemon fragrance oil and 8 drops yellow colorant. Pour into pre-pared 2.5" tube mold. Set and release.
2. Cut yellow soap column into six sections. Place in prepared 3.25" mold. Cool.
3. Melt 2 oz. of clear glycerin soap base. Add 4 drops white colorant. Pour in and around cooled sections. Set and release.
4. Trim ends and slice soap into two 3/4" thick bars.

Recipe 136
Pink Grapefruit Slice

Makes two bars, 3/4" thick.

Melt & Pour Base: 8 oz. clear glycerin soap base

Fragrance: 20 drops pink grapefruit

Colorant: 5 drops red, 5 drops white

Molds: 2.5" tube, 3.25" tube

See "Tube Molded Soaps" in the Designer Techniques section and follow these instructions:

1. Melt 6 oz. of clear glycerin soap base. Add 20 drops pink grapefruit fragrance oil, 1 drop white colorant, and 5 drops red colorant. Pour into prepared 2.5" tube mold. Set and release.
2. Cut pink soap column into six sections, and place in prepared 3.25" mold. Cool.
3. Melt 2 oz. of clear glycerin soap base. Add 4 drops white colorant. Pour in and around cooled sections. Set and release.
4. Trim ends and slice soap into two 3/4" thick bars.

Recipe 137
Peppermint Twist

You can make this peppermint twist soap in red or green or both. This recipe makes 2 bars, 1" thick.

Melt & Pour Base: 6 oz. clear glycerin soap base

Fragrance: 10 drops spearmint (for green twist) or 10 drops cinnamon (for red twist)

Colorant: 4 drops green (for green twist) or 4 drops red (for red twist)

Molds: 2" round tube

See "Tube Molded Soaps" in the Designer Techniques section and follow these instructions:

1. Pour 3 oz. clear soap base with cinnamon fragrance and red colorant (for red twist) or spearmint fragrance and green colorant (for green twist) in a prepared 2" round tube mold. Let set and release.
2. Cut soap columns into 8 sections. Place four sections back in the prepared 2" round mold. Pour 3 oz. clear soap base with 4 drops white colorant. Let set and release.
3. Trim soap and slice into two 1" thick bars.

Recipe 138
Candy Corn

Makes two bars, 1" thick.

Melt & Pour Base: 6 oz. clear glycerin soap base

Fragrance: 15 drops sugar cookie, 10 drops brown sugar

Colorant: 4 drops white, 4 drops yellow, 3 drops China mustard

Molds: 3" heart tube

See "Tube Molded Soaps" in the Designer Techniques section and follow these instructions:

1. Pour 6 oz. clear soap base with 4 drops white colorant and 10 drops sugar cookie fragrance oil into a prepared 3" heart tube mold. Let set and release.
2. Cut 1" piece from bottom of heart column and place it back into mold.
3. Re-melt the remaining soap, adding 4 drops yellow colorant and 10 drops brown sugar fragrance oil. Pour into prepared heart mold. Let set and release.
4. Cut a 3/4" slice from the top of the heart soap column and set aside. Place the larger bottom section of heart back in heart mold.
5. Re-melt the set aside piece of remaining soap and add 3 drops china mustard colorant and 5 drops sugar cookie fragrance oil. Pour into heart mold. Let set and release.
6. Trim and slice soap into two 1" thick bars.

Recipe 139
Peppermint Stick

Makes two 3" tube bars.

Melt & Pour Base: 3 oz. clear glycerin soap base

Fragrance: 15 drops candy cane

Colorant: 3 drops white, 2 drops red, 2 drops green

Molds: .75" round tube mold

See "Layered Soaps" and "Tube Molded Soaps" in the Designer Techniques section and follow these instructions:

1. Place prepared .75" round tube mold in a cup. Prop the mold so it rests at a 45-degree angle.
2. Pour in 1 oz. clear soap base with 3 drops white colorant and 5 drops candy cane fragrance oil. Let set.
3. Pour in 1 oz. clear soap base with 2 drops red colorant and 5 drops candy cane fragrance oil. Let set.
4. Pour in 1 oz. clear soap base with 2 drops green colorant and 5 drops candy cane fragrance oil. Let set.
5. Repeat layers, letting set between each. When completely set, release the soap and cut in half to create two 3" soap tubes.

Recipe 140
Whimsical Checkered

Makes two bars.

Melt & Pour Base: 5 oz. clear glycerin soap base, 5 oz. whitened glycerin soap base

Fragrance: 10 drops buttercream, 10 drops ylang-ylang

Colorant: 5 drops yellow, 3 drops blue

Molds: Two 5-oz. square molds

See "Soaps with Defined Color Areas" in the Designer Techniques section and follow these instructions:

1. Pour the whitened glycerin soap base with 5 drops yellow colorant and 10 drops buttercream fragrance in one of the molds. Let set and release.
2. Cut the bar with angled lines to create 16 pieces. Carefully arrange every other piece in one of the molds. Arrange the remaining pieces in the second mold.
3. Pour the clear glycerin soap base with 5 drops blue colorant and 10 drops ylang-ylang fragrance in the empty spaces in each mold. Let set and release.

135

134

133

136

Scrubbing Soaps

Recipes #141 and 142 are made by pouring melted soap base around a slice of loofah (a natural vegetable sponge that is a member of the squash plant family). A round tube mold makes a perfectly circular soap — just place the loofah slice in the mold and pour the melted soap in and around it.
Let set and release, then trim the ends.

Recipe 141
Natural Loofah Rounds

Makes two slices, 1" thick.

Melt & Pour Base: 6 oz. clear glycerin soap base (3 oz. per slice of loofah)

Fragrance: 10 drops chamomile

Additives: Two slices, 1" thick, of natural loofah

Molds: Round molds or round tube molds to fit loofah slices

See "Soaps with Embedded Sponges" in the Designer Techniques section.

Recipe 142
Colored Loofah Rounds

Makes two slices, one of each color.

Melt & Pour Base: 6 oz. clear glycerin soap base (3 oz. per slice)

Fragrance: 10 drops green apple (for green slice), 10 drops raspberry (for pink slice)

Additives: 1" slice green dyed loofah, 1" slice pink dyed loofah

Molds: 2 round molds or 2 round tube molds to fit loofah slices

See "Soaps with Embedded Sponges" in the Designer Techniques section.

Recipe 143
Pink Loofah Shapes

Makes two 1" slices.

Melt & Pour Base: 6 oz. clear glycerin soap base (3 oz. per slice)

Fragrance: 20 drops strawberry

Additives: Pinch of iridescent powder, two 1" slices pink dyed loofah

Molds: 3" heart tube, 3" blossom tube

See "Soaps with Embedded Sponges" in the Designer Techniques section and the instructions above this section.

Recipe 144
Colored Loofah Shapes

Makes two slices.

Melt & Pour Base: 6 oz. clear glycerin soap base (3 oz. per slice)

Fragrance: 20 drops herbal mint

Additives: 1" slices green dyed loofah

Molds: 3" butterfly tube, 3.5" oval tube

See "Soaps with Embedded Sponges" in the Designer Techniques section and the instructions above this section.

TIPS

- It is much easier to cut the loofah into slices **before** pouring in the soap rather than placing a whole loofah in the mold and slicing it after the soap has set.

- Recipes #143 and 144 are made by molding the loofah sponges into shapes. To make shapes, soak the loofah slice in hot water for 10 minutes. Place the softened sponge into a shaped tube mold. Let dry overnight before preparing the mold and pouring in the melted soap.

141

142

144

144

143

Hanging Soaps

The Soap Tassel™ is the creative novelty of master soap maker Sandy Maine. If you add extra fragrance to the soap beads, you can use them as air fresheners.

Recipe 145
Pickles and Olive Soap Tassel™

Melt & Pour Base: 6 oz. clear glycerin soap base

Fragrance: 10 drops lime

Colorant: 8 drops green, 2 drops white, 1 drop red

Molds: .75" round tube, 1.5" blossom tube

Other Supplies: 36" thin yellow satin ribbon, plastic straw

See "Soap Beads" in the Designer Techniques section and follow these instructions:

1. **Olives:** Push a straw into the prepared base of .75" round tube mold. Pour in 1 oz. clear soap base with 3 drops green, 2 drops white, and 1 drop red colorant to make an olive hue. Let set. Pull out straw and fill hole with 1/2 oz. soap base with 1 drop red colorant. Set and release. Slice to make olives.
2. **Pickles:** Melt remainder and base and add 5 drops green. Mold in the blossom tube. Slice the soap column with a garnish knife to make the pickles.
3. Thread the soap beads on the ribbon.

Recipe 146
Pink Soap Tassel™

Melt & Pour Base: 6 oz. *each* clear, whitened, and pink-colored glycerin soap base

Fragrance: 10 drops rose, 10 drops baby powder

Colorant: 5 drops blue

Molds: 3-oz. rectangle, 1.5" heart tube

Other Supplies: 24" thin white satin ribbon

See "Soap Beads" in the Designer Techniques section and follow these instructions:

1. Make a layered bar in the rectangle mold with the white and blue-colored base and baby powder fragrance. Let set and release. Cut 1.5" cubes from the layered soap.
2. Cut 1" cubes from the pink soap base (no molding necessary).
3. Mold white base and rose fragrance in heart tube. Let set, release, and slice.
4. Thread the soap beads on the ribbon.

Recipe 147
Floral Soap Tassel™

Melt & Pour Base: 6 oz. *each* whitened and clear glycerin soap base

Fragrance: 10 drops honeysuckle

Colorant: 3 drops green, 10 drops yellow

Molds: .75" round tube, 1.5" heart tube, 1.5" blossom tube

Other Supplies: Red soap paint, 24" thin yellow satin ribbon

See "Soap Beads" and "Painted Soaps" in the Designer Techniques section and follow these instructions:

1. Mold white and yellow blossoms. Slice. Accent each blossom soap bead with a dot of red paint.
2. Mold green base in the heart tube. Set and slice. Cut the green heart in half to create the leaves.
3. Mold yellow base in the round tube.
4. Thread the soap beads on the ribbon.

Recipe 148
Star Soap Tassel™

Melt & Pour Base: 6 oz. *each* clear and whitened glycerin soap base

Fragrance: 10 drops musk

Colorant: yellow, blue

Molds: .75" round tube, 1.5" star tube

Other Supplies: 24" thin yellow satin ribbon

See "Soap Beads" in the Designer Techniques section. Thread the soap beads on the ribbon.

146

147

145

148

Stacked Shapes

Stacked soaps are easy and fun to make from soap sheets, which you can purchase or make yourself from melt and pour soap base. See "Stacked Shapes" in the Designer Techniques section. The shapes can be cut with cookie cutters.

Recipe 149
Stars

Soap Sheets: Red, blue, white, green

Cutters: Small star, large star, falling star

See "Stacked Shapes" in the Designer Techniques section.

To make the Patriotic Star, stack a large blue star, a large white star, a large red star, and a small blue star.

To make the Falling Star, stack a large white star, a blue falling star, a green falling star, and a white small star.

Recipe 150
Flowers

Soap Sheets: Red, green, yellow

Cutters: Large star, large petaled flower, small petaled flower

See "Stacked Shapes" in the Designer Techniques section.

To make the Red Flower, stack a yellow large star, a green large petaled flower (cut into five leaf shapes), a red large petaled flower, and a yellow small petaled flower.

To make the Yellow Flower, stack a yellow large petaled flower, a green large petaled flower (cut into five leaf shapes), a yellow large petaled flower, and a red small petaled flower.

Recipe 151
Rainbow Circle

Soap Sheets: Red, yellow, green, blue

Cutters: Large round

See "Stacked Shapes" in the Designer Techniques section.

To make the Rainbow, stack a red circle, a yellow circle, a green circle, and a blue circle.

Recipe 152
Rainbow Arch

Soap Sheets: Red, yellow, green, blue

Other Supplies: Rubber band

See "Stacked Shapes" in the Designer Techniques section.

To make the Rainbow Arch, Cut a 3/4" x 5" strip from each color. Heat and stack the strips. While still warm, form into an arch and secure with a rubber band to hold the shape while the soap cools. If needed, trim the ends at an angle to finish.

Treasure Soaps

Treasure soaps have items molded in the soap. When the soap is used up, the treasure remains. These make great gifts for kids.

Recipe 153
Happy Face Treasure

Makes one bar.

Melt & Pour Base: 1 oz. fluorescent pink soap base, 1 oz. clear glycerin soap base

Fragrance: 10 drops strawberry

Molds: 2 oz. round dome

Other Supplies: Happy face flower erasers

See "Embedded Soaps" in the Designer Techniques section.

Recipe 154
Tropical Fish Treasure

Makes one bar.

Melt & Pour Base: 1 oz. whitened glycerin soap base, 1 oz. clear glycerin soap base

Fragrance: 10 drops mango

Colorant: 3 drops purple

Molds: 2 oz. round dome

Other Supplies: Tropical fish erasers

See "Embedded Soaps" in the Designer Techniques section.

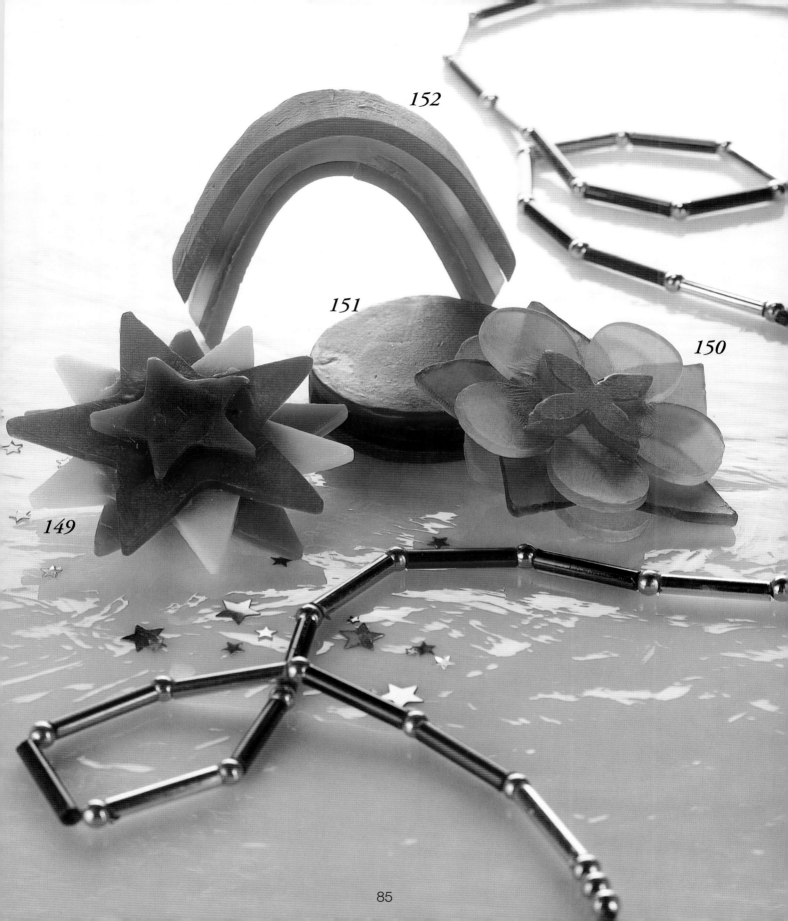

152

151

150

149

Recipe 155
Butterfly Treasure

Makes one bar.

Melt & Pour Base: 1 oz. whitened glycerin soap base, 2 oz. clear glycerin soap base

Fragrance: 15 drops papaya

Colorant: 3 drops blue

Molds: 3 oz. round oval

Other Supplies: Plastic butterfly

See "Embedded Soaps" in the Designer Techniques section.

Recipe 156
Frog Treasure

Makes one bar.

Melt & Pour Base: 1 oz. whitened glycerin soap base, 2 oz. clear glycerin soap base

Fragrance: 15 drops grapefruit

Colorant: 4 drops green

Additives: Pinch of iridescent powder

Molds: 2 oz. round dome

Other Supplies: Plastic frog

See "Embedded Soaps" in the Designer Techniques section.

Recipe 157
Dino in a Dino

This recipe, courtesy Environmental Technologies, makes one bar.

Melt & Pour Base: 2 oz. clear glycerin soap base

Fragrance: 10 drops dewberry

Colorant: 2 drops green

Molds: 2-oz. dinosaur

Other Supplies: Plastic dinosaur

See "Embedded Soaps" in the Designer Techniques section.

Recipe 158
Rubber Ducky

This recipe, courtesy Environmental Technologies, makes one bar.

Melt & Pour Base: 2 oz. clear glycerin soap base

Fragrance: 10 drops baby powder

Colorant: 2 drops blue

Treasure: Rubber ducky

Molds: 2-oz. round

Other Supplies: Rubber ducky

See "Embedded Soaps" in the Designer Techniques section. Float the rubber ducky on the soap right after pouring.

Recipe 159
Floral Bright

Makes two bars.

Melt & Pour Base: 5 oz. clear glycerin soap base

Fragrance: 15 drops lily of the valley, 10 drops rain

Additives: Pinch of iridescent powder, silk flower petals with all hard plastic pieces removed

Molds: 2.5" tube mold, 3" tube mold

See "Tube Molded Soaps" and "Embedded Soaps" in the Designer Techniques section. Pour the soap base in the prepared tube molds, then push in silk flower petals. Let set, release, and trim.

159

Soaps in Soap

Many small soaps, such as the shapes made with tray molds, can be used as additives or embeds in larger bars. You make small molded soaps using many of the recipes in this book or purchase them. Then you place the small soaps in a larger mold and add clear glycerin soap. When hardened, you can see the embedded shapes.

Recipe 160
Ocean Motifs

Makes two bars.

Melt & Pour Base: 6 oz. clear glycerin soap base

Fragrance: 15 drops ocean breeze

Additives/Embeds: Molded sea motif soaps in blue, white, green

Molds: 3-oz. rectangle

See "Soaps in Soap" in the Designer Techniques section.

Recipe 161
Sparkling Snowflakes

Makes two bars.

Melt & Pour Base: 6 oz. clear glycerin soap base

Fragrance: 15 drops winterberry

Additives/Embeds: Molded snowflake soaps with iridescent powder

Molds: 3-oz. round

See "Soaps in Soap" in the Designer Techniques section.

Recipe 162
Funky Lemon

Makes one bar.

Melt & Pour Base: 3 oz. clear glycerin soap base

Fragrance: 15 drops Lemon

Additives/Embeds: Double molded lemon soap

Molds: 3-oz. oval

See "Soaps in Soap" in the Designer Techniques section.

158

160

161

162

Bagged Soaps

Bagged soaps contain colorful pieces of soap or toys or other items with clear soap base poured around them. They are molded in a plastic bag that also is their packaging. When ready to use, they are removed from the plastic bag.

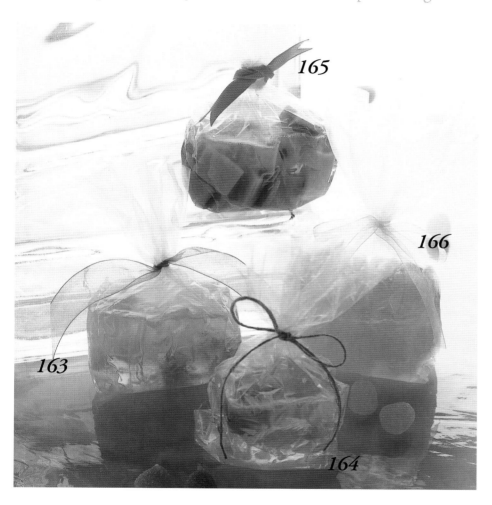

Recipe 163
Jellies Candy Bag

Melt & Pour Base: 6 oz. clear glycerin soap base

Fragrance: 10 drops raspberry, 10 drops green apple

Embeds: Red, pink, yellow, white, blue soap cubes

Molds: Plastic bag set in a tube mold

See "Bagged Soaps" in the Designer Techniques section.

Recipe 164
Goldfish in Bag

Melt & Pour Base: 6 oz. clear glycerin soap base

Fragrance: 15 drops rain

Embeds: 2 plastic goldfish

Molds: Plastic bag set in a tube mold

See "Bagged Soaps" in the Designer Techniques section.

Recipe 165
Licorice Candy Bag

Melt & Pour Base: 6 oz. clear glycerin soap base

Fragrance: 15 drops aniseed

Embeds: layered "all sorts" soaps pieces – see below

Molds: Plastic bag set in a tube mold

See "Bagged Soaps" in the Designer Techniques section and follow these instructions:

1. Make the layered licorice candies by layering orange, black, and yellow soap base in a 3-oz. rectangle mold. Cut in 1" cubes when set.
2. Make round licorice, but with black centers in yellow and pink rounds.

Recipe 166
Candy Hearts

Melt & Pour Base: 6 oz. clear glycerin soap base

Fragrance: 10 drops cinnamon, 10 drops strawberry

Embeds: White, pink, and red heart-shaped soap slices

Molds: Plastic bag set in a tube mold

See "Bagged Soaps" in the Designer Techniques section.

Fizzy Soaps

These combinations of fizzing bath salts and scented soaps are delightful to use and fun to make.

Recipe 167
English Rose Bath Fizzy Soap

For the soap:

Melt & Pour Base: 4 oz. clear glycerin soap base

Fragrance: 10 drops English rose

Colorant: 5 drops red

Molds: 2-oz. rectangle

For the bath fizzy:

Bath Salts: 1/2 cup mixed fizzy bath salts

Fragrance: 10 drops vanilla

Other Supplies: Small silk rosebud

See "Fizzy Soaps" in the Designer Techniques section and follow these instructions:

1. Mold the soap. Let set and release.
2. Mix fizzy bath salts and vanilla fragrance oil.
3. Mold the bath salts around the soap bars, packing the salts firmly to hold. Let harden.
4. Accent the top with a small silk rosebud.

Recipe 168
Chocolate Tub Truffle

For the soap:

Melt & Pour Base: 3 oz. whitened glycerin soap base

Fragrance: 10 drops chocolate, 5 drops vanilla

Colorant: 5 drops red

Molds: 1.5" heart tube mold

For the bath fizzy:

Bath Salts: 1/2 cup mixed fizzy bath salts

Fragrance: 10 drops vanilla

Additives: 1 teaspoon cocoa butter

Molds: 1-oz. heart

See "Fizzy Soaps" in the Designer Techniques section and follow these instructions:

1. Make the soap. Let set and release. Slice 1/2" thick.
2. Mix the salts.
3. Place a small amount of salts in the bottom of the 1-oz. heart mold. Add a slice of heart-shaped soap. Fill the mold with more salts. Pack down the salts firmly. Release on a piece of cardboard to dry and harden.

Recipe 169
Vanilla Cream Bath Fizzy Soap

For the soap:

Melt & Pour Base: 2 oz. clear glycerin soap base

Fragrance: 5 drops vanilla cream

Colorant: 3 drops blue

Molds: 1/2-oz. disk

For the bath fizzy:

Bath Salts: 1/2 cup mixed fizzy bath salts

Fragrance: 10 drops vanilla cream

Colorant: 5 drops orange

Molds: 2-oz. star with face

See "Fizzy Soaps" in the Designer Techniques section and follow these instructions:

1. Make the soap. Let set and release.
2. Mix the salts.
3. Place a small amount of salts in the bottom of the star mold. Add a soap disk. Fill the mold with more salts. Pack down the salts firmly. Release on a piece of cardboard to dry and harden.

Recipe 170
Orange Spice Bath Fizzy Soap

The photo shows how the soap looks that is inside the fizzy soap ball.

For the soap:

Melt & Pour Base: 3 oz. coconut oil soap base

Fragrance: 10 drops cinnamon orange

Colorant: 3 drops orange

Molds: 3-D round

For the bath fizzy:

Bath Salts: 1/2 cup mixed fizzy bath salts

Fragrance: 10 drops cinnamon orange

Colorant: 5 drops orange

Additives: 1/2 teaspoon cinnamon powder

Other Supplies: Whole cloves

See "Fizzy Soaps" in the Designer Techniques section and follow these instructions:

1. Make the soap. Let set and release.
2. Mix the salts.
3. Mold the salts around round soap ball, packing the salts firmly to hold.
4. Accent the top with a single whole clove.

170

168

167

169

Embedded Soaps

The soaps in this section use pieces of soap from soap sheets and pieces cut from soap scraps to embellish larger soap bars. They are a good way to use up your leftovers.

Recipe 171
Cucumber Peel

Makes two bars.

Melt & Pour Base: 8 oz. clear glycerin soap base

Fragrance: 20 drops cucumber

Additives: White and green soap curls cut from soap sheets

Molds: 4-oz. rectangle

See "Soaps in Soap" in the Designer Techniques section.

Recipe 172
Ocean Curls

Makes two bars.

Melt & Pour Base: 8 oz. opaque blue-colored glycerin soap base

Fragrance: 15 drops ocean breeze

Colorant: 4 drops blue

Additives: Soap curls cut from clear glycerin soap base

Molds: 4-oz. rectangle

See "Soaps in Soap" in the Designer Techniques section.

Recipe 173
Heart Swirl

Makes two bars.

Melt & Pour Base: 5 oz. clear glycerin soap base

Fragrance: 10 drops bayberry spice

Colorant: 3 drops red

Additives: Purple opaque soap noodles, pink opaque soap noodles

Molds: 2-oz. heart, 3 oz. heart

See "Soaps in Soap" in the Designer Techniques section.

Recipe 174
Curls

Makes two bars.

Melt & Pour Base: 6 oz. whitened glycerin soap base

Fragrance: 10 drops blueberry

Additives: Red soap curls, blue soap curls

Molds: 3-oz. oval

See "Soaps in Soap" in the Designer Techniques section.

178

177   175

176

Recipe 175
Triangles

Makes two bars – cut the square in half diagonally.

Melt & Pour Base: 5 oz. whitened glycerin soap base

Fragrance: 10 drops dewberry

Additives: Green, yellow, and red soap curls cut from soap sheets

Molds: 5-oz. square

See "Soaps in Soap" in the Designer Techniques section.

Recipe 176
Marbles

Makes two marble bars.

Melt & Pour Base: 6 oz. clear glycerin soap base

Fragrance: 15 drops bubblegum

Additives: Scraps from multi-colored soap sheets

Molds: 3-D round

See "Soaps in Soap" in the Designer Techniques section and follow these instructions:
1. Use soap sheet scraps to fill each side of the two-part 3-D round mold.
2. Pour in the clear, fragrant soap base. Let set and release.

Recipe 177
Multi-Colored

Makes one bar.

Melt & Pour Base: 4 oz. clear glycerin soap base

Fragrance: 10 drops apricot

Additives: Scraps from multi-colored soap sheets

Molds: 4-oz. rectangle

See "Soaps in Soap" in the Designer Techniques section.

Recipe 178
Funky Flower

Makes one bar.

Melt & Pour Base: 3 oz. clear glycerin soap base

Fragrance: 8 drops honeysuckle

Additives: Soap flower cut from blue soap sheet with large petaled flower cutter

Molds: 2.5" round tube

See "Soaps in Soap" in the Designer Techniques section. Cut a slice with a garnish knife to accent.

Dip-Dot Painted Soaps

Dip-Dot Painting is an easy technique for embellishing your soaps.

Recipe 179
Dip-Dot Rose

Makes two bars.

Melt & Pour Base: 6 oz. opaque pink-colored soap base

Fragrance: 10 drops Victorian rose

Molds: 3-oz. round

See "Painted Soaps" in the Designer Techniques section.

Recipe 180
Dip-Dot Lavender

Makes two bars.

Melt & Pour Base: 6 oz. opaque lavender-colored soap base

Fragrance: 10 drops lavender

Molds: 3-oz. rectangle

See "Painted Soaps" in the Designer Techniques section.

Recipe 181
Dip-Dot Daisy

Makes two bars.

Melt & Pour Base: 8 oz. opaque blue-colored soap base

Fragrance: 10 drops china rain

Molds: 4-oz. oval

See "Painted Soaps" in the Designer Techniques section.

Recipe 182
Dip-Dot Hollyhock

Makes one bar.

Melt & Pour Base: 5 oz. opaque yellow-colored soap base

Fragrance: 10 drops lily of the valley

Molds: 5-oz. square

See "Painted Soaps" in the Designer Techniques section.

180

182

179

181

Shower Soaps

These soaps are handy in the shower – you can hang them in the shower, eliminating the need for a soap dish.

186

Recipe 183
Carved Soap-on-a-Rope

Makes one.

Melt & Pour Base: 5 oz. clear glycerin soap base

Fragrance: 20 drops lilac

Colorant: 23 drops blue, 3 drops green, 2 drops white (for a translucent teal hue)

Additives: Clear green and purple soap chunks, 36" nylon rope

Molds: 3" oval tube mold

See "Chunk Style Soaps" and "Carved Soaps" in the Designer Techniques section and follow these instructions:
1. Make soap. Let set and release.
2. Carve soap into a rough oval shape.
3. Thread a large needle with a piece of thread. Loop the nylon cord through the thread and pull both the thread and the nylon cord through the soap.
4. Discard thread. Tie the cord in a knot to hold soap.

Recipe 184
Orange Soap-on-a-Rope

Makes one.

Melt & Pour Base: 8 oz. coconut oil soap base

Fragrance: 20 drops orange cinnamon

Colorant: 5 drops China mustard

Additives: 36" green nylon cord, 1 silk leaf

Molds: Large 3-D round candle mold

Other Supplies: Plastic straw

Follow these instructions:
1. Make soap. Pour soap in mold. Clamp the two-part mold together with the plastic straw in the center.

Let set and release.
2. Pull out the straw, create a hole through the soap ball. Thread the green cord through the hole and knot the ends.
3. Cut a small hole in the end of the silk leaf and thread on the cording to the top of the soap ball.

Recipe 185
Shell Soap-on-a-Rope

Makes one.

Melt & Pour Base: 4 oz. coconut oil soap base

Fragrance: 10 drops coconut, 10 drops jasmine

Colorant: 6 drops blue

Additives: 36" white nylon cord

Molds: 4-oz. rubber shell mold

Follow these instructions:
Place the knotted end of the cord in the melted soap after the soap is poured in the mold. Let set and release.

Recipe 186
Rain Shower Mobile

Makes one. This mobile combines slices from three tube molded soaps.

Soaps: 1 rainbow tube mold bar, 1 cloud tube mold bar, and 4 raindrop tube mold bars with colors and scents of your choice

Other Supplies: Three 16" pieces white satin ribbon

See "Tube Molded Soaps" and "Soap Beads" in the Designer Techniques section. Thread the soap slices together to form a mobile.

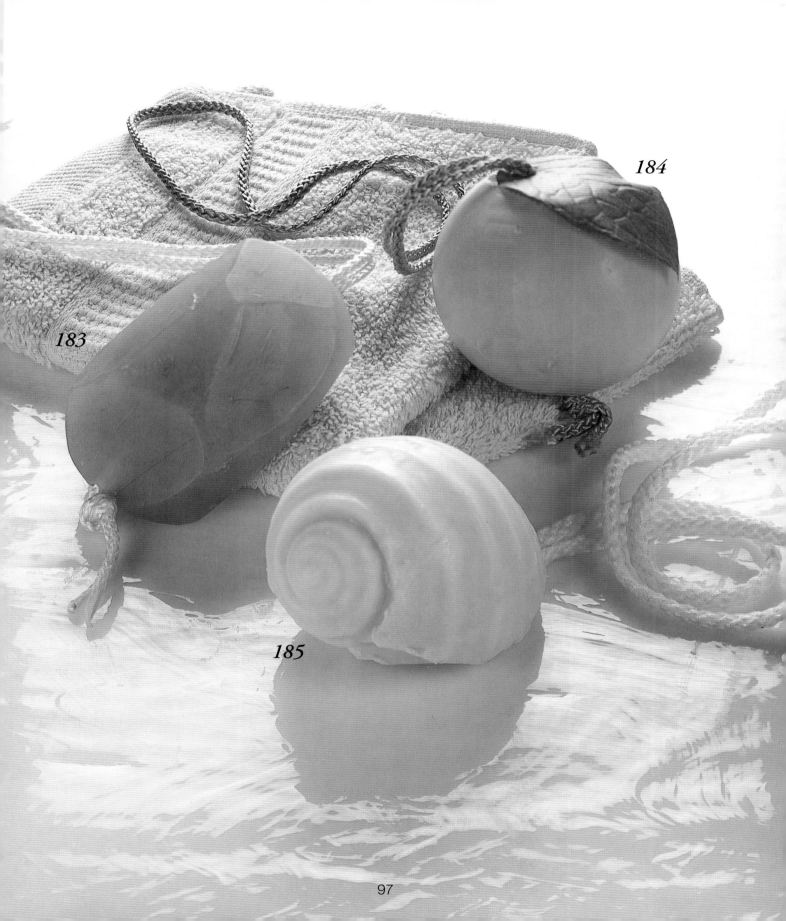

183

184

185

Leaf & Petal Soaps

The following four recipes are super simple and use very little soap base. Individual silk petals or leaves are dipped in fragrant clear soap base and placed on a sheet of wax paper to set. Each dipped petal is good for one hand washing, and the petal is discarded after use. CAUTION: Use only the soft silken part of the petal or leaf; remove any hard plastic pieces before dipping in the soap.

Recipe 187
Rose Petals

Melt & Pour Base: 2 oz. clear glycerin soap base

Fragrance: 10 drops rose

Base: 10 to 12 individual silk rose petals

Recipe 188
Fall Leaves

Melt & Pour Base: 2 oz. clear glycerin soap base

Fragrance: 10 drops buttery maple

Base: 10 to 12 silk oak leaves

Recipe 189
Herbal Leaves

Melt & Pour Base: 2 oz. clear glycerin soap base

Fragrance: 10 drops herbal mint

Base: 10 to 12 green silk leaves

Recipe 190
Floral Petals

Melt & Pour Base: 2 oz. clear glycerin soap base

Fragrance: 10 drops lilac

Base: 6 to 8 whole silk daisy petals

Carved, Cut & Shaped Soaps

This section features more ideas for unusual shapes and combinations.

Recipe 191
Funky Dots

Makes two bars.

Melt & Pour Base: 6 oz. clear glycerin soap base

Fragrance: 20 drops apple-pear

Colorant: 3 drops green, 3 drops red

Molds: 3-oz. oval

Other Supplies: Melon baller

Follow these instructions:
1. Mold a green bar with 3 oz. soap base, 10 drops fragrance oil, and green colorant. Let set and release.
2. Mold a red bar with 3 oz. soap base, 10 drops fragrance oil, and red colorant. Let set and release.
3. With a melon baller, scoop out a ball of soap from each bar.
4. Pour a bit of melted clear soap base in the holes. Place the red soap ball in the hole in the green bar and the green soap ball in the hole in the red bar.

Recipe 192
Funky Stripes

Makes two bars.

Melt & Pour Base: 6 oz. clear glycerin soap base, 2 oz. whitened glycerin soap base

Fragrance: 10 drops Christmas

Colorant: 3 drops green, 3 drops red

Molds: 3-oz. rectangle

Follow these instructions:
1. Mold a green bar with 3 oz. soap base, 5 drops fragrance oil, and green colorant. Let set and release.
2. Mold a red bar with 3 oz. soap base, 5 drops fragrance oil, and red colorant. Let set and release.
3. Cut each bar diagonally into three pieces.
4. Trim each straight cut edge with a garnish cutter. Place soap pieces back in the molds, reversing the colors on the middle stripes.
5. Pour the melted white soap base into the spaces. Let set and release.

Continued on page 100

187

190

189

188

Recipe 193
Crayon Soap

Makes four crayon soaps.

Melt & Pour Base: 3 oz. coconut oil soap base

Fragrance: Blueberry, strawberry

Colorant: 30 drops blue, 30 drops red

Molds: 1.75" plastic tube mold

See "Tube Molded Soaps" in the Designer Techniques section and follow these instructions:

1. Pour 1.5 oz. of blue colored, blueberry scented soap in the prepared mold. Let set and release.
2. Pour 1.5 oz. of red colored, strawberry scented soap in the prepared mold. Let set and release.
3. Cut each soap tube in half to make 3" crayons. "Sharpen" one end to a point with a knife to finish.

Recipe 194
Moldable Soap

Using coconut oil soap base and mixing the soap as it cools make this recipe work. The cornstarch keeps the soap from hardening into a solid bar, and the added glycerin gives elasticity. Kids love to play with this soap in the tub because it can be rolled and molded as they bathe.

Melt & Pour Base: 4 oz. coconut oil soap base

Fragrance: 10 to 20 drops pineapple, sweet orange, or strawberry

Colorant: 4 to 8 drops yellow, orange, or red

Additives: 1 heaping tablespoon of cornstarch (plus extra cornstarch for mixing), 1-1/2 tablespoons liquid glycerin

Follow these instructions:

1. Mix the cornstarch, liquid glycerin, fragrance oil, and colorant together in a small glass bowl.
2. Melt the soap base. Mix in the colored and scented cornstarch mixture.
3. With a fork, stir the soap until it cools and starts to set up.
4. Turn the soap out on a piece of wax paper that has been sprinkled with cornstarch.
5. Coat your hands with a small amount of cornstarch and gently knead your cooled soap until smooth, with no hardened soap bits. If the soap starts to stick to your hands, sprinkle cornstarch on your hands and the soap.

Borrowed Soaps

I've borrowed the recipes for the next four soaps from two talented soapmakers, Maria Nerius, author of *Soapmaking for Fun and Profit* (Prima Publishing, and Katie Hacker author of *Natural Soapmaking* (Hot Off the Press Publications).

Recipe 195
Ron's Refreshing Raspberry

Recipe courtesy of my good friend Maria Nerius.

Makes two bars.

Melt & Pour Base: 6 oz. coconut oil base, 1 oz. clear glycerin soap base

Fragrance: 10 drops chocolate, 15 drops raspberry, 5 drops peppermint

Colorant: 4 drops coffee (for a soft tan hue), 2 drops red

Molds: 3" blossom plastic tube

Other Supplies: Melon baller

See "Tube Molded Soaps" in the Designer Techniques section and follow these instructions:

1. Make soap, let set, release, and slice.
2. Use a melon baller to scoop out a hole in the middle of the bar. Fill the hole with melted clear soap base colored with 2 drops red colorant.

Recipe 196
Jim's Jeweled Jelly

Recipe courtesy of my good friend Maria Nerius.

Makes two bars.

Melt & Pour Base: 4 oz. clear glycerin soap base

Additives: Scented pink, white, red, blue, yellow soap cubes

Molds: 2.5" round plastic tube mold

See "Chunk Style Soaps" in the Designer Techniques section.

Recipe courtesy of soap crafter Katie Hacker.

Makes two bars.

Melt & Pour Base: 5 oz. avocado cucumber glycerin soap base

Fragrance: 2 drops relaxing blend, 2 drops romantic blend of your choice

Colorant: 4 drops blue

Molds: Two 3 oz. round domes

Follow these instructions:

1. Melt 2.5 oz. of the soap, add the relaxing fragrance, and pour into the mold. Let set and release.
2. Cut a 3/8" strip out of the center. Place the strip in the center of one mold and the two side pieces in the other mold.
3. Melt the remaining soap. Add the romantic fragrance and blue colorant. Pour into the molds. Let set and release.
4. Trim the soaps with a sharp knife, if needed.

CREAMY SOAPS

Recipe 199
Butter Bar

Makes two bars.

Melt & Pour Base: 8 oz. coconut oil soap base

Fragrance: 10 drops buttercream

Colorant: 4 drops yellow

Additives: 1 teaspoon shea butter, 1/2 teaspoon cocoa butter, 1 teaspoon citric acid

Molds: 4-oz. rectangle

See the Basic Technique. Melt shea butter and cocoa butter. Mix in citric acid. Stir well. Add to melted soap base.

Recipe 197
Better Halves

Recipe courtesy of soap crafter Katie Hacker.

Makes two bars.

Melt & Pour Base: 5 oz. avocado cucumber glycerin soap base

Colorant: 4 drops green colorant

Additives: 1/4 teaspoon *each* of dried eucalyptus, lemongrass, mint and chamomile. 1/2 teaspoon ground apricot seed

Molds: Two 3 oz. rounds

Follow these instructions:

1. Melt 2.5 oz. of the soap and stir in half of the additives. Pour into a mold and let set.
2. Release from mold and cut in half. Place half in each of two molds.
3. Melt the remaining soap and stir in remaining additives. Add green colorant and pour in each mold. Let cool and release.

199

197

198

201

Recipe 200
Cocoa Butter Soap

Makes two bars.

Melt & Pour Base: 8 oz. glycerin soap base with added goat's milk

Fragrance: 15 drops cocoa butter

Additives: 1 teaspoon cocoa butter, 3 capsules vitamin E

Molds: 4-oz. southwest motifs

See the Basic Technique.

Recipe 201
Angel Soft

Makes four guest-size bars.

Melt & Pour Base: 6 oz. coconut oil soap base

Fragrance: 15 drops milk 'n honey

Additives: 1/2 teaspoon powdered buttermilk, 1 teaspoon honey, 1/2 teaspoon citric acid

Molds: Small fancy shapes

Other Supplies: Angel motif soap decals

See "Soaps with Decals" in the Designer Techniques section.

Creamy Soaps

Additives such as dried milk powder and cocoa butter lend a creamy texture to your soap.

Recipe 202
Coffee Cream

Makes two bars.

Melt & Pour Base: 3 oz. clear glycerin soap base, 3 oz. whitened glycerin soap base

Fragrance: 10 drops espresso (in clear base), 10 drops vanilla cream (in white base)

Colorant: 4 drops coffee (in clear base)

Additives: 1/2 teaspoon whole milk powder, 2 capsules vitamin E, 1 teaspoon liquid glycerin (to white base)

Molds: 3-oz. round

Other Supplies: Whole coffee beans, soap beveler

See "Marbled Soaps" and "Soaps with Decorative Accents" in the Designer Techniques section. Bevel the edges with a soap beveler and accent with a whole coffee bean.

Recipe 203
Creamy Almond

Makes two bars.

Melt & Pour Base: 6 oz. glycerin soap base with added goat's milk

Fragrance: 10 drops almond milk

Colorant: 4 drops sand (for a light tan hue)

Additives: 1/2 teaspoon powdered whole milk and 1/2 teaspoon almond meal mixed in 1 teaspoon liquid glycerin

Molds: 3-oz. oval

See the Basic Technique.

Recipe 204
Rosemary Cream

Makes three bars.

Melt & Pour Base: 5 oz. glycerin soap base with added olive oil and suspension formula

Fragrance: 10 drops rosemary

Additives: 1/2 teaspoon dried rosemary, 1/2 teaspoon powdered whole milk, 1 teaspoon liquid glycerin

Molds: 1.5-oz. guest rectangle with embossing

See the Basic Technique.

Recipe 205
Avocado Cucumber Cream

Makes two slices, 1" thick.

Melt & Pour Base: 4 oz. avocado cucumber glycerin soap base with suspension formula

Fragrance: 20 drops aloe vera

Additives: 1/2 teaspoon shea butter, 1/2 teaspoon-powdered goat's milk, 1 teaspoon liquid glycerin, 6 drops grapefruit seed extract

Molds: 2.5" round tube mold

Other Supplies: Green soap sheet

See "Tube Molded Soaps" in the Designer Techniques section. Line mold with green soap sheet before pouring.

Recipe 206
Berries 'n Cream

Makes two bars.

Melt & Pour Base: 3 oz. whitened glycerin soap base, 3 oz. clear glycerin soap base

Fragrance: 10 drops strawberry (to whitened base), 10 drops raspberry (to clear base)

Colorant: 4 drops red (to clear base)

Additives: 1/2 teaspoon whole milk powder and 1 teaspoon liquid glycerin (to clear base)

Molds: 3 oz. round

See "Marbled Soaps" in the Designer Techniques section.

209

206

208

205

210

Therapeutic Soaps

These refreshing soaps are great additions to a home spa. The heavenly aromas will relax and refresh.

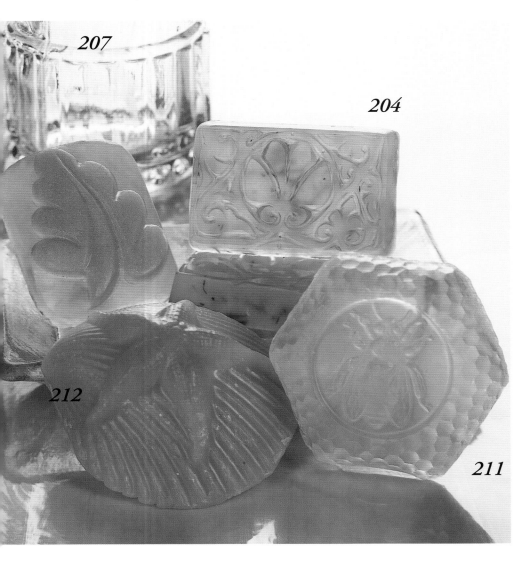

Recipe 208
Spa Therapy

This recipe is courtesy Environmental Technologies. It makes two bars.

Melt & Pour Base: 6 oz. coconut oil soap base

Fragrance: 10 drops cocoa butter, 4 drops coconut

Colorant: 2 drops sand (for a cream hue)

Additives: 2 natural sea sponges (to fit inside 3 oz. round mold)

Molds: 3 oz. round

See "Soaps with Embedded Sponges" in the Designer Techniques section.

Recipe 209
Ocean Spa

Makes two bars.

Melt & Pour Base: 7 oz. whitened glycerin soap base

Fragrance: 10 drops bay rum, 5 drops lime, 5 drops mixed spice

Colorant: 5 drops blue

Additives: 1/2 teaspoon palm oil, 1/2 teaspoon coconut oil

Molds: 3.5-oz. two dolphins

See the Basic Technique.

Recipe 210
Bali Spa Soap

Makes two bars.

Melt & Pour Base: 3 oz. whitened glycerin soap base

Fragrance: 5 drops mango, 5 drops coconut

Additives: 1 teaspoon powdered milk powder, 1 teaspoon coconut oil

Molds: 1.5 oz. round flourish

See the Basic Technique.

Recipe 207
Mountain Therapy

Makes two guest-size bars.

Melt & Pour Base: 3 oz. clear glycerin soap base

Fragrance: 5 drops pine, 5 drops violet, 5 drops vanilla

Colorant: 2 drops green (to 2 oz. of soap base)

Additives: Pinch of gold luster powder (to 1 oz. of soap base)

Molds: 1.5 oz. leaf motif

See "Soaps with Defined Color Areas" (pour-and-scrape) in the Designer Techniques section.

Mood Soaps

The following soaps were designed with shapes, colors, and scents to reflect their names. The fragrances used can help alter your mood.

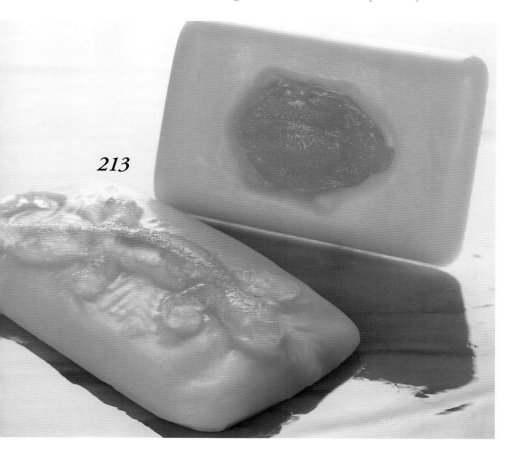

213

Recipe 213
Revitalize

Makes two bars.

Melt & Pour Base: 1 oz. clear glycerin soap base, 3 oz. whitened glycerin soap base

Fragrance: 10 drops rosemary, 5 drops peppermint

Colorant: 2 drops green (to clear soap base), 3 drops yellow and 1 drop green (to white soap base)

Molds: 2-oz. rectangle molds with embossed frog and lizard

See "Soaps with Defined Color Areas" (pour-and-scrape) in the Designer Techniques section.

Recipe 214
Uplifting

Makes one bar.

Melt & Pour Base: 3 oz. glycerin soap base with added goat's milk

Fragrance: 10 drops vanilla, 6 drops sweet orange

Molds: 3-oz. angel

See the Basic Technique.

Recipe 215
Romantic

Makes one bar.

Melt & Pour Base: 4 oz. clear glycerin soap base

Fragrance: 10 drops rose, 5 drops clove, 5 drops ylang-ylang

Colorant: 4 drops red, 1 drop black (for a wine hue)

Molds: 4 oz. embossed heart

See the Basic Technique.

Recipe 211
Nourishing

Makes two bars.

Melt & Pour Base: 6 oz. clear glycerin soap base with added olive oil

Fragrance: 10 drops ylang-ylang, 10 drops rose

Molds: 3-oz. bee and honeycomb mold

See the Basic Technique.

Recipe 212
Invigorating

Makes two bars.

Melt & Pour Base: 6 oz. clear glycerin soap base

Fragrance: 10 drops peppermint, 15 drops sweet orange

Colorant: 3 drops blue, 3 drops green (for a clear teal hue)

Molds: 3-oz. clam shell (clam shell with starfish design)

See "Soaps with Defined Color Areas" (pour-and-scrape) in the Designer Techniques section.

Recipe 218
Dreaming

Makes two bars.

Melt & Pour Base: 7 oz. whitened glycerin soap base

Fragrance: 10 drops lavender, 15 drops chamomile

Colorant: 4 drops blue (in 6 oz. soap base)

Molds: 4-oz. rectangle and 3-oz. rectangle with moon and stars embossed

See "Soaps with Defined Color Areas" (pour-and-scrape) in the Designer Techniques section.

Recipe 219
Warming

Makes one bar.

Melt & Pour Base: 4 oz. whitened glycerin soap base

Fragrance: 10 drops ginger, 10 drops vanilla

Colorant: 2 drops sand (to 3 oz. soap base), 2 drops orange (to 1 oz. soap base)

Molds: 4 oz. round with sun motif

See "Soaps with Defined Color Areas" (pour-and-scrape) in the Designer Techniques section.

Recipe 220
Healing

Make two bars.

Melt & Pour Base: 8 oz. whitened glycerin soap base

Fragrance: 15 drops aloe vera, 10 drops rose

Colorant: 4 drops orange, 2 drops red (for a coral hue)

Additives: 2 capsules vitamin E, 1 teaspoon aloe vera gel

Molds: 3.75-oz. rose

See the Basic Technique.

Recipe 216
Playful

Makes two guest-size bars.

Melt & Pour Base: 4 oz. whitened glycerin soap base

Fragrance: 10 drops vanilla, 10 drops watermelon, 5 drops rose

Colorant: 2 drops orange (to 3 oz. soap base)

Molds: 1.5-oz. fish round

See "Soaps with Defined Color Areas" (pour-and-scrape) in the Designer Techniques section.

Recipe 217
Escape

Makes one bar.

Melt & Pour Base: 4 oz. clear glycerin soap base

Fragrance: 6 drops lavender, 10 drops vanilla, 5 drops patchouli

Colorant: 4 drops blue

Molds: 4-oz. rubber shell mold

See the Basic Technique.

214

216

220

Recipe 221
Comforting

Makes one bar.

Melt & Pour Base: 3 oz. clear glycerin soap base

Fragrance: 6 drops vanilla, 5 drops jasmine

Colorant: 3 drops orange

Molds: 3-oz. butterfly

See the Basic Technique.

Recipe 222
Serenity Now

Makes one bar.

Melt & Pour Base: 4.25 oz. clear glycerin soap base

Fragrance: 10 drops sweet orange,
5 drops patchouli

Colorant: 4 drops green

Molds: 4.25-oz. arabesque

See the Basic Technique.

226

225

226

223

Recipe 223
Winter Celebrations

Makes two bars, 1" thick.

Melt & Pour Base: 10 oz. clear glycerin soap base

Fragrance: 5 drops *each* cinnamon, sweet orange, hazelnut, vanilla

Colorant: 3 drops green, 6 drops white, 1 drop red

Molds: 1.5" star tube, 2.5" round tube

Other Supplies: 3 plastic straws

See "Tube Molded Soaps" in the Designer Techniques section and follow these instructions:

1. Pour 3 oz. clear glycerin soap base with 3 drops green and 2 drops white in a prepared 1.5" star tube mold. Let set and release. Cut the star in half vertically to create the holly leaves.
2. Push three plastic straws in the prepared base of a 2.5" round tube mold. Position the cooled green soap columns. Pour in 6 oz. clear soap base with 4 drops white colorant and all the fragrance oils. Let set.
3. Pull out the straws. Pour 1 oz. clear glycerin soap base with 1 drop red colorant in the holes. Let set and release.
4. Trim and slice into two 1" thick slices.

Recipe 224
Summer Days

Makes one bar.

Melt & Pour Base: 3 oz. whitened glycerin soap base

Fragrance: 5 drops *each* watermelon, vanilla, cantaloupe

Colorant: 4 drops blue

Molds: 3-oz. rectangle

Other Supplies: Soap decal with blueberries

See "Soaps with Decals" in the Designer Techniques section.

Recipe 225
Sparkling

Makes two bars.

Melt & Pour Base: 1 oz. whitened glycerin soap base, 6 oz. clear glycerin soap base

Fragrance: 10 drops spearmint, 10 drops winterberry (to clear soap base)

Additives: Pinch of silver glitter

Molds: 3 oz. embossed star

See "Soaps with Defined Color Areas" (pour-and-scrape) in the Designer Techniques section.

Recipe 226
Snowball

Melt & Pour Base: 4 oz. frosting soap

Fragrance: 10 drops peppermint (added to the frosting soap)

Additives: 1" and 1-1/2" diameter soap balls carved from clear blue glycerin soap base

Other Supplies: Iridescent powder

See "Carved Soaps" in the Designer Techniques section and #280 Frosted Petit Fours. Cover the blue soap balls with frosting soap, packing it on firmly, as if you were making a real snowball. Sprinkle the finished soaps with a pinch of iridescent powder. Let dry 24 hours before using.

Recipe 227
Peaceful

Makes two bars.

Melt & Pour Base: 8 oz. whitened glycerin soap base

Fragrance: 10 drops vanilla, 10 drops sandalwood

Colorant: 4 drops blue (to 6 oz. soap base)

Molds: 4-oz. oval with embossed peace dove

See "Soaps with Defined Color Areas" (pour-and-scrape) in the Designer Techniques section.

Recipe 228
Mystical

Makes two bars.

Melt & Pour Base: 1 oz. whitened glycerin soap base, 6 oz. clear glycerin soap base

Fragrance: 10 drops green tea, 5 drops cinnamon

Colorant: 4 drops red, 3 drops blue (to clear soap base)

Molds: 3 oz. round with embossed southwest motifs

See "Soaps with Defined Color Areas" (pour-and-scrape) in the Designer Techniques section.

Recipe 229
Tranquility

Makes one bar.

Melt & Pour Base: 1 oz. whitened glycerin soap base, 4 oz. opaque green-colored glycerin soap base

Fragrance: 10 drops honeysuckle, 6 drops jasmine, 6 drops musk, 6 drops mandarin

Molds: 4 oz. round with embossed Chinese character

See "Soaps with Defined Color Areas" (pour-and-scrape) in the Designer Techniques section.

Recipe 230
Relaxing

Makes one bar.

Melt & Pour Base: 4 oz. whitened glycerin soap base

Fragrance: 8 drops lavender, 8 drops ylang-ylang

Colorant: 2 drops blue (to 3 oz. soap base)

Molds: 3-oz. rectangle with embossed motif

See "Soaps with Defined Color Areas" (pour-and-scrape) in the Designer Techniques section.

229

219

TRANQUILITY

228

Embossed Soaps

The soaps in this section are embossed with rubber stamps or soap stamps. This creative technique allows you to create a soap that can look elegant or funky – depending on the design you choose to emboss.

Recipe 231
Air

Makes one bar.

Melt & Pour Base: 4 oz. clear glycerin soap base

Fragrance: 5 drops bergamot, 10 drops lemon

Additives: Pinch of iridescent glitter

Molds: 4-oz. rectangle

Other Supplies: Rubber stamp

See "Embossed Soaps" in the Designer Techniques section.

Recipe 232
Water

Makes one bar.

Melt & Pour Base: 4 oz. clear glycerin soap base

Fragrance: 10 drops ylang-ylang, 5 drops bergamot

Colorant: 3 drops blue, 2 drops green (for a clear teal hue)

Additives: Pinch of iridescent glitter

Molds: 4-oz. rectangle

Other Supplies: Rubber stamp

See "Embossed Soaps" in the Designer Techniques section.

Recipe 233
Fire

Makes one bar.

Melt & Pour Base: 3 oz. clear glycerin soap base

Fragrance: 5 drops cinnamon, 5 drops ginger

Colorant: 3 drops red

Additives: Red and yellow soap cubes, pinch of iridescent powder

Molds: 4-oz. rectangle

Other Supplies: Rubber stamp

See "Embossed Soaps" and "Chunk Style Soaps" in the Designer Techniques section.

Recipe 234
Earth

Makes one bar.

Melt & Pour Base: 4 oz. whitened glycerin soap base

Fragrance: 10 drops pine, 5 drops sandalwood, 5 drops patchouli

Colorant: 3 drops green, 1 drop orange (for a moss green hue)

Additives: 1/4 teaspoon wheat bran, 1/4 teaspoon dried mint leaves

Molds: 4-oz. rectangle

Other Supplies: Rubber stamp

See "Embossed Soaps" in the Designer Techniques section.

Recipe 235
Classic Embossed

Makes one bar.

Melt & Pour Base: 5 oz. clear glycerin soap base

Fragrance: 10 drops amber romance

Colorant: 3 drops red, 2 drops white (for a translucent pink hue)

Molds: 5-oz. square

Other Supplies: Gold luster powder (to highlight embossed motif), rubber stamp

See "Embossed Soaps" in the Designer Techniques section.

Recipe 236
Tuscany Embossed

Makes one bar.

Melt & Pour Base: 3 oz. whitened glycerin soap base

Fragrance: 10 drops pear

Colorant: 3 drops blue, 2 drops red

Molds: 3-oz. oval

Other Supplies: Gold luster powder (to highlight embossed motif), rubber stamp

See "Embossed Soaps" in the Designer Techniques section.

233

234

231

232

Recipe 237
Pear Embossed

Makes two bars.

Melt & Pour Base: 6 oz. whitened glycerin soap base

Fragrance: 15 drops pear, 5 drops mixed spice

Colorant: 3 drops green, 2 drops yellow, 1 drop orange (for a ripe pear hue)

Molds: 3-oz. rectangle

Other Supplies: Pear motif soap stamp

See "Stamped Soaps" in the Designer Techniques section.

Recipe 238
Bee Embossed

Makes two bars.

Melt & Pour Base: 6 oz. whitened glycerin soap base

Fragrance: 10 drops honey

Colorant: 3 drops yellow, 1 drop black (for a deep amber hue)

Molds: 3-oz. hexagon

Other Supplies: Bee motif soap stamp

See "Stamped Soaps" in the Designer Techniques section.

Soap Gems and Stones

The following soap gems were molded in 2" round tube molds, cut into 2" slices, and carved to make the gems. The crystal gems have sharp, angled cuts; the smooth gems were cut, then polished smooth with a terrycloth towel. Other techniques were used to make the marbled soap projects.

Recipe 240
Rose Quartz

Makes two soap gems.

Melt & Pour Base: 3 oz. clear glycerin soap base

Fragrance: 10 drops rose petals

Additives: White and pink soap cubes, pinch of iridescent powder

Molds: 2" round plastic tube

See "Chunk Style Soaps" and "Carved Soaps" in the Designer Techniques section.

Recipe 241
Jade

Makes two soap gems.

Melt & Pour Base: 3 oz. clear glycerin soap base

Fragrance: 10 drops jasmine, 5 drops herbal

Additives: Opaque green soap cubes with green tea, pinch of gold luster powder

Molds: 2" round plastic tube

See "Chunk Style Soaps" and "Carved Soaps" in the Designer Techniques section. Polish smooth.

Recipe 242
Milky Quartz

Makes two soap gems.

Melt & Pour Base: 3 oz. clear glycerin soap base

Fragrance: 10 drops milk 'n honey

Additives: White and clear soap cubes, pinch of pearl luster powder

Molds: 2" round plastic tube

See "Chunk Style Soaps" and "Carved Soaps" in the Designer Techniques section.

Recipe 239
Amethyst

Makes two soap gems.

Melt & Pour Base: 3 oz. clear glycerin soap base

Fragrance: 10 drops blue musk

Additives: Blue and purple soap cubes, pinch of silver glitter

Molds: 2" plastic round tube

See "Chunk Style Soaps" and "Carved Soaps" in the Designer Techniques section.

Recipe 243
Opal

Makes two soap gems.

Melt & Pour Base: 3 oz. clear glycerin soap base

Fragrance: 10 drops eucalyptus therapy

Additives: Blue, pink, and white soap cubes, pinch of pearl luster powder

Molds: 2" round plastic tube

See "Chunk Style Soaps" and "Carved Soaps" in the Designer Techniques section.

Recipe 244
Star Sapphire

Makes two bars.

Melt & Pour Base: 6 oz. whitened glycerin soap base, 2 oz. clear glycerin soap base

Fragrance: 10 drops neroli

Colorant: 6 drops blue (to white soap base)

Additives: Pinch of pearl luster powder (added to 2 oz. clear soap base)

Molds: 4-oz. round, 3-oz. oval dome

See "Chunk Style Soaps" in the Designer Techniques section and follow these instructions:

Technique: carved, polished
1. Pour the blue soap base in the molds. Let set and release.
2. Carve the tops of the soaps deeply with a star design.
3. Melt clear soap base and add pearl luster powder. Pour 1 oz. pearl soap base in the bottom of each mold. Immediately place the soap bars in the molds. Press down firmly to force the liquid soap into the carved areas. Let set and release.
4. Polish the soap stones with a terry-cloth towel to reveal the star pattern.

247

248

244

246

243

245

249

254

253

Recipe 245
Amber

Makes two soap gems.

Melt & Pour Base: 3 oz. clear glycerin soap base

Fragrance: 10 drops amber romance

Additives: Olive oil base soap cut into cubes, pinch of gold luster powder, a few black plastic ants

Molds: 2" round plastic tube

See "Chunk Style Soaps" and "Carved Soaps" in the Designer Techniques section. Polish smooth.

Recipe 246
Turquoise

Makes two soap gems.

Melt & Pour Base: 3 oz. clear turquoise-colored soap base

Fragrance: 10 drops musk

Additives: Purple, green, and blue soap cubes

Molds: 2" round plastic tube

See "Chunk Style Soaps" and "Carved Soaps" in the Designer Techniques section. Polish smooth.

Recipe 247
Diamond

Makes two soap gems.

Melt & Pour Base: 3 oz. clear glycerin soap base

Fragrance: 10 drops lily of the valley

Additives: Clear soap cubes, pinch of iridescent powder

Molds: 2" round plastic tube

See "Chunk Style Soaps" and "Carved Soaps" in the Designer Techniques section.

Recipe 248
Emerald

Makes two soap gems.

Melt & Pour Base: 3 oz. clear green-colored soap base

Fragrance: 10 drops spearmint

Additives: Green and clear soap cubes, pinch of iridescent glitter

Molds: 2" round plastic tube

See "Chunk Style Soaps" and "Carved Soaps" in the Designer Techniques section.

Recipe 249
Sedimentary Layered

This soap is made from the leftover soap you have after filling a mold. It makes two soap gems.

Melt & Pour Base: Leftover melted soap from other recipes

Fragrance: A variety of scents

Molds: 2" round plastic tube

See "Tube Molded Soaps" and "Carved Soaps" in the Designer Techniques section and follow these instructions:

Prepare the tube mold. As you work, add small amounts of melted soap. Try to keep the colors coordinated for a more realistic appearance.

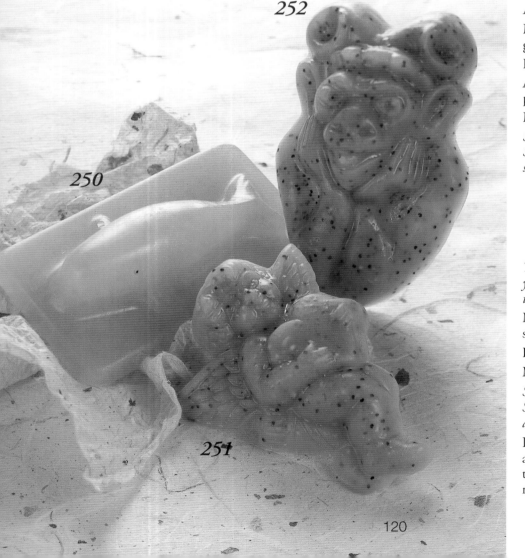

255

260

256

Recipe 250
Antique Ivory

Makes one bar.

Melt & Pour Base: 1.5 oz. clear glycerin soap base, 1.5 oz. whitened glycerin soap base

Fragrance: 10 drops vanilla

Additives: Pinch of gold luster powder (to clear soap base)

Molds: 3-oz. rectangle with three-dimensional whale

See "Marbled Soaps" in the Designer Techniques section.

Recipe 251
Granite Angels

Makes two bars.

Melt & Pour Base: 5 oz. whitened glycerin soap base with added coconut oil

Fragrance: 15 drops mulberry

Colorant: 3 drops black (for a gray hue)

Additives: 1/2 teaspoon tapioca, 1/4 teaspoon poppy seeds

Molds: 3-oz. and 2 oz. angel

See the Basic Technique.

Recipe 252
Granite Gargoyle

Makes one bar.

Melt & Pour Base: 4.25 oz. whitened glycerin soap base with added coconut oil

Fragrance: 10 drops cinnamon, 5 drops ginger

Colorant: 3 drops black (for a gray hue)

Additives: 1/2 teaspoon tapioca, 1/4 teaspoon poppy seeds

Molds: 4.25-oz. gargoyle

See the Basic Technique.

Recipe 253
Sand Pebble Soap

Make three pebble soaps.

Melt & Pour Base: 2 oz. whitened glycerin soap base with added coconut oil

Fragrance: 6 drops earth

Colorant: 3 drops sand

Additives: 1/4 teaspoon wheat germ, 1/4 teaspoon paprika

Molds: Rubber pebble molds

See the Basic Technique.

Recipe 254
Gray Pebble Soap

Makes two pebble soaps.

Melt & Pour Base: 2 oz. whitened glycerin soap base with added coconut oil

Fragrance: 6 drops earth

Colorant: 2 drops black

Additives: Pinch *each* of tapioca, poppy seeds

Molds: Rubber pebble molds

See the Basic Technique.

Recipe 255
Purple Crystal

Makes two soap crystals.

Melt & Pour Base: 4 oz. clear glycerin soap base, 5 oz. whitened glycerin soap base

Fragrance: 10 drops blackberry

Colorant: 4 drops blue, 2 drops red

Additives: 1/2 teaspoon rock salt

Molds: 1-oz. and 4-oz. round dome

Other Supplies: Melon baller

See "Layered Soaps" in the Designer Techniques section and follow these instructions:

1. Pour 5 oz. whitened soap base with blackberry fragrance in the mold. Let set.
2. With a melon baller, carefully scoop out all but a 1/2" rim of white soap.
3. Pour 3-1/2 oz. clear soap base with 2 drops blue and 2 drops red colorant. Let set.
4. Scoop out all but 1/4" of the soap.
5. Re-melt the white soap base. Add 2 drops red colorant to make it pink and pour in the mold. Let set.
6. Scoop out a small hole in the center. Add the rock salt and pour in the last of the clear soap base. Let set and release.
7. Trim and polish.

Recipe 256
Pink Crystal

Makes one soap crystal.

Melt & Pour Base: 4 oz. clear glycerin soap base, 4 oz. whitened glycerin soap base

Fragrance: 5 drops apricot, 4 drops strawberry

Colorant: 2 drops red

Additives: 1/2 teaspoon rock salt

Molds: 4-oz. round dome

See "Layered Soaps" in the Designer Techniques section and follow the instructions for #255 Purple Crystal, making the layers white, opaque pink, opaque purple, and clear.

Recipe 257
Iceberg Bar

Makes one bar.

Melt & Pour Base: 3 oz. clear glycerin soap base

Fragrance: 5 drops eucalyptus, 6 drops peppermint, 6 drops spearmint

Colorant: 1 drop white

Additives: Clear soap chunks with iridescent glitter

Molds: 4-oz. dome

See "Chunk Style Soaps" in the Designer Techniques section.

Recipe 258
Childhood

Melt & Pour Base: 2 oz. opaque blue-colored glycerin soap base, 4 oz. opaque yellow-colored glycerin soap base

Fragrance: 5 drops baby powder (to blue soap base), 10 drops baby powder (to yellow soap base)

Molds: 3-D block, rubber duck

See the Basic Technique.

Recipe 259
Marbled Sea Shells

Makes four bars.

Melt & Pour Base: 4 oz. whitened glycerin soap base

Fragrance: 10 drops ocean breeze

Colorant: 4 drops blue (to 2 oz. of soap base)

Molds: Sea shell motif tray

See "Marbled Soaps" in the Designer Techniques section.

123

Recipe 260
Carved Marble

Makes one bar.

Melt & Pour Base: 6 oz. clear glycerin soap base

Fragrance: 15 drops gardenia

Colorant: 3 drops pink luster (to 3 oz. soap base), 4 drops red and 6 drops purple (to 3 oz. soap base)

Molds: 5-oz. square

See "Marbled Soaps" and "Carved Soaps" in the Designer Techniques section.

Recipe 261
Fruit Punch Marbled

Makes four bars.

Melt & Pour Base: 2 oz. whitened glycerin soap base, 2 oz. clear glycerin soap base.

Fragrance: 5 drops sweet orange and 4 drops melon (to whitened soap base), 5 drops strawberry and 4 drops mango (to clear base)

Colorant: 3 drops melon (to 2 oz. whitened base), 2 drops red (to 2 oz. clear base)

Molds: Fruit motifs tray

See "Marbled Soaps" in the Designer Techniques section.

Recipe 262
Lena's Blue Fish

Lena, my 15-year-old daughter, developed this recipe for her signature soap. It makes three bars.

Melt & Pour Base: 5 oz. clear glycerin soap base

Fragrance: 10 drops Hawaiian rain (in 2.5 oz. soap base), 10 drops earth (in 2.5 oz. soap base)

Colorant: 2 drops blue (in 2.5 oz. soap base), 3 drops blue luster (in 2.5 oz. soap base)

Molds: 1.5-oz. fish

See "Marbled Soaps" in the Designer Techniques section.

Soothing Soaps

Use these recipes for soaps that soothe and rejuvenate. All these soaps are easy to make using the basic "Melt & Pour" technique.

Recipe 263
Lemongrass Mint Massage

This recipe is courtesy Katie Hacker. It makes one bar.

Melt & Pour Base: 2.5 oz. avocado cucumber soap base with suspension formula

Fragrance: 2 drops lemongrass

Additives: 1/4 teaspoon lemongrass, 1/4 teaspoon dried mint leaves

Molds: 2.5-oz. hexagon massage

See the Basic Technique.

Recipe 264
Apricot Massage

This recipe is courtesy Katie Hacker. It makes one bar.

Melt & Pour Base: 3.75 oz. glycerin soap base with added olive oil and suspension formula

Fragrance: 2 drops chamomile

Additives: 1 teaspoon ground apricot seed

Molds: 3.75-oz. rectangle massage

See the Basic Technique.

Recipe 265
Scott's Sporting Soap

This is the healing and soothing soap my husband enjoys after a day on the Lacrosse field. This recipe makes one bar.

Melt & Pour Base: 1 oz. whitened glycerin soap base, 3 oz. clear glycerin with added hemp oil

Fragrance: 5 drops earth, 3 drops pine, 3 drops spearmint

Additives: 1 teaspoon peppermint (to clear glycerin soap base)

Molds: 4-oz. rectangle massage

See "Soaps with Defined Color Areas" (pour-and-scrape) in the Designer Techniques section.

Recipe 266
Fresh Massage Bar

Makes one bar.

Melt & Pour Base: 3-oz. glycerin soap base with added hemp oil

Fragrance: 5 drops eucalyptus, 5 drops peppermint

Molds: 3-oz. round massage

See the Basic Technique.

Christmas Soaps

These soap recipes are just for the holidays.
They make great gifts.

Recipe 267
Christmas Guest

Makes four bars.

Melt & Pour Base: 4 oz. coconut oil soap base

Fragrance: 6 drops eggnog

Molds: Fancy small bar shapes

Other Supplies: 4 Christmas-themed soap decals

See "Soaps with Decals" in the Designer Techniques section.

Recipe 268
Santa Christmas Gift

Makes two bars.

Melt & Pour Base: 2 oz. clear glycerin soap base

Fragrance: 5 drops candy cane

Colorant: 2 drops red

Accent: 2 Santa erasers

Molds: 1-oz. heart

See "Embedded Toy Soaps" and "Soaps with Decorative Accents" in the Designer Techniques section.

Recipe 269
Snowflake Christmas Gift

Makes two soaps.

Melt & Pour Base: 2 oz. whitened glycerin soap base

Fragrance: 3 drops mandarin, 2 drops cinnamon, 2 drops vanilla

Colorant: 2 drops blue

Accent: 2 snowflake erasers

Molds: 1-oz. petit four shape

See "Embedded Toy Soaps" and "Soaps with Decorative Accents" in the Designer Techniques section.

Recipe 270
Christmas

Makes two bars.

Melt & Pour Base: 5 oz. clear glycerin soap base, 1 oz. whitened glycerin soap base

Fragrance: 3 drops chocolate, 3 drops peppermint, 3 drops vanilla

Colorant: 3 drops red (in clear soap base)

Molds: Christmas motifs tray

See "Soaps with Defined Color Areas" (pour-and-scrape) in the Designer Techniques section.

270

269

268

Shampoo & Scrub Bars

These special soaps are cleansing bars. The shampoo bars are great all-purpose bars to make for travel or camping because they can be used on both hair and body.

Recipe 271
Shampoo Bar

This blend is good for oily hair. The recipe makes two bars.

Melt & Pour Base: 4 oz. glycerin soap base with added olive oil

Fragrance: 10 drops rosemary, 10 drops lemon

Molds: 4-oz. rectangle

To make two bars, cut rectangle in half and bevel the edges.

Recipe 272
Dandruff Shampoo Bar

While I am not convinced this works, it's worth a try! The recipe makes two bars.

Melt & Pour Base: 4 oz. coconut oil soap base

Additives: 3 capsules vitamin E, 1 teaspoon aloe vera gel, 2 crushed aspirins

Molds: 4-oz. rectangle

To make two bars, cut rectangle in half and bevel the edges.

Recipe 273
Brown Sugar Scrub

Sugar scrubs are all the rage at expensive spas! This recipe makes two bars.

Melt & Pour Base: 6 oz. whitened glycerin soap base

Fragrance: 15 drops brown sugar

Colorant: 5 drops orange

Additives: 3 teaspoons brown sugar, 1 teaspoon palm oil

Molds: 3-oz. radiant heart

See the Basic Technique.

Recipe 274
Salt Polishing Bar

A luxurious scrub in a fragrant bar! This recipe makes two bars.

Melt & Pour Base: 4 oz. coconut oil soap base

Fragrance: 10 drops mango, 10 drops mandarin

Additives: 2 teaspoons fine sea salt, 1 teaspoon shea butter, 2 capsules vitamin E

Molds: 1.5-oz. dome, 2-oz. flourish round

See the Basic Technique.

Soap Sweets

The soaps in this section look good enough to eat – but don't try.

Recipe 275
Lemon Soap Tart

Makes two soap tarts.

Melt & Pour Base: 1 oz. whitened glycerin soap base, 2 oz. clear glycerin soap base

Fragrance: 5 drops vanilla, 10 drops lemon

Colorant: 1 drop sand, 1 drop white, 3 drops yellow

Accent: Small amount of frosting soap (See #280 Frosted Petit Fours.)

Molds: 1-oz. metal tart pan

See "Layered Soaps" in the Designer Techniques section and assemble this way:
First layer - Whitened glycerin soap base with sand colorant and vanilla fragrance
Second layer - Clear glycerin with white and yellow colorants and lemon fragrance
Topping - Frosting soap

Recipe 276
Very Berry Soap Tart

Makes two soap tarts.

Melt & Pour Base: 1 oz. whitened glycerin soap base, 2 oz. clear glycerin soap base

Fragrance: 5 drops vanilla, 10 drops strawberry shortcake

Colorant: 1 drop sand, 2 drops red

Additives: Clear red soap cubes cut with a garnish knife

Accent: Small amount of frosting soap (See #280 Frosted Petit Fours.)

Molds: 3-oz. metal tart pan

See "Layered Soaps" in the Designer Techniques section and assemble this way:
First layer - Whitened glycerin soap base with sand colorant and vanilla fragrance
Second layer - Clear glycerin soap base with red colorant and strawberry shortcake fragrance poured over clear red soap cubes
Topping - Frosting soap

274

272

267

273

279

261

Recipe 277
Coconut Cream Soap Tart

Makes two soap tarts.

Melt & Pour Base: 1 oz. whitened glycerin soap base,
2 oz. clear glycerin soap base

Fragrance: 5 drops vanilla, 10 drops coconut

Colorant: 1 drop sand, 2 drops white

Additives: 1/2 teaspoon dried coconut

Accent: Small amount of frosting soap (See #280 Frosted
Petit Fours.)

Molds: 3-oz. metal heart-shaped tart pan

*See "Layered Soaps" in the Designer Techniques section and
assemble this way:*
First layer - Whitened glycerin soap base with sand colorant
and vanilla fragrance
Second layer -Clear glycerin soap base with white colorant,
coconut fragrance, and dried coconut
Topping - Frosting soap

276

278

277

275

Recipe 278
Peppermint Patty

Makes two bars.

Melt & Pour Base: 4 oz. clear glycerin soap base

Fragrance: 10 drops chocolate mint

Colorant: 6 drops coffee, 2 drops green

Molds: 2 oz. round dome

See "Layered Soaps" in the Designer Techniques section and assemble this way:

First layer - 1 oz. soap base with 3 drops coffee colorant and 5 drops chocolate mint fragrance
Second layer - 2 oz. soap base with green colorant
Third layer - 1 oz. soap base with 3 drops coffee colorant and 5 drops chocolate mint fragrance

Recipe 279
Fruit Cocktail

This chunk style bar can easily be made in a larger loaf mold, and all loaf-style recipes can be converted to mold individual bars this way. This recipe makes two bars.

Melt & Pour Base: 4 oz. clear glycerin soap base

Fragrance: 5 drops pineapple, 5 drops orange, 5 drops pink grapefruit

Embeds: Orange slices and pink grapefruit slices cut from tube soaps, pineapple chunks cut from yellow glycerin soap base, cherries cut from red soap molded in a .75" round tube mold

Molds: 3-oz. rectangle

See "Chunk Style Soaps" in the Designer Techniques section. Fill the molds with the colored soap pieces and pour the fragrant melted soap over them.

Recipe 280
Frosted Petit Fours

This petit four technique is courtesy Yaley Enterprises and shows off the company's frosting soap base, which comes in a 9-oz. loaf. The recipe makes four small bars.

Melt & Pour Base: 4 oz. whitened glycerin soap base

Fragrance: 6 drops of your choice

Colorant: 3 drops of your choice

Molds: 1-oz. petit four

Other Supplies: Frosting soap, pastry bag and tip

Pour whitened glycerin base with colorant and fragrance added into molds. Let set and release. Frost soap "cakes" with frosting soap, following these instructions:

1. Divide the frosting loaf into four equal 2.25 oz. pieces. Cut up one piece of soap into small pieces and melt in a 4-cup heat-resistant glass measuring cup.
2. Add a few drops colorant (e.g., green for leaves, red for flowers). Whip the soap on low speed, using an electric mixer, while adding 2 teaspoons water. Continue whipping on medium speed until the soap becomes dry, thick, and fluffy (approximately 3 to 4 minutes – the more you whip it, the fluffier it gets and the easier it is to work with.)
3. Place the whipped soap in a pastry bag with the tip of your choice and use it to decorate individual petit four soaps. Allow 24 hours for the frosting to dry.

Recipe 281
Red Heart Petit Fours

Makes four small bars.

Melt & Pour Base: 4 oz. whitened glycerin soap base

Fragrance: 6 drops strawberry shortcake

Colorant: 3 drops red

Molds: heart-shaped 1-oz. petit four

Other Supplies: Frosting soap, pastry bag and tip

Pour whitened glycerin base with colorant and fragrance added. Let set and release. Frost soap "cakes" with frosting soap, following instructions for #280, above.

Recipe 282
Yellow Petit Fours

Makes four small bars.

Melt & Pour Base: 4 oz. whitened glycerin soap base

Fragrance: 3 drops lemon, 3 drops vanilla

Colorant: 3 drops yellow

Molds: 1-oz. petit four

Other Supplies: Frosting soap, pastry bag and tip

Pour whitened glycerin base with colorant and fragrance added. Let set and release. Frost soap "cakes" with frosting soap, following instructions for #280, above.

Recipe 283
Blue Petit Fours

Makes four small bars.

Melt & Pour Base: 4 oz. whitened glycerin soap base

Fragrance: 3 drops vanilla, 3 drops cake bake

Colorant: 3 drops blue

Molds: 1-oz. petit four

Other Supplies: Frosting soap, pastry bag and tip

Pour whitened glycerin base with colorant and fragrance added. Let set and release. Frost soap "cakes" with frosting soap, following instructions for #280, above.

281

283

Creative Molded Soaps

The first two tube soap recipes use a two-part tube mold from Martin Creative. The molds make detailed soap columns and can make up to 18 soap bars when completely filled. The remaining soaps in this section showcase other molding techniques.

Recipe 284
Creative Cameo

Makes two slices, 3/4" thick.

Melt & Pour Base: 3 oz. clear glycerin soap base, 3 oz. whitened glycerin soap base

Fragrance: 4 drops frankincense, 10 drops gardenia, 6 drops vanilla

Colorant: 8 drops blue (4 drops to each base)

Molds: 2-part cameo tube mold, 2.5" round tube mold

See "Tube Molded Soaps" in the Designer Techniques section.

Recipe 285
Creative Duck

Makes two slices, 3/4" thick.

Melt & Pour Base: 3 oz. clear glycerin soap base, 3 oz. whitened glycerin soap base

Fragrance: 12 drops baby powder, 5 drops rose, 4 drops vanilla

Colorant: 5 drops yellow (in white soap base), 4 drops blue (in clear base)

Molds: 2-part duck tube mold, 2.5" round tube mold

See "Tube Molded Soaps" in the Designer Techniques section.

Recipe 286
Jon's Green Frog

Jonathan, my 11-year-old son, developed this soap with lots of his favorite scents. It makes one bar.

Melt & Pour Base: 4 oz. clear glycerin soap base

Fragrance: 20 drops sweet orange, 15 drops lime

Colorant: 5 drops green

Molds: 4-oz. rubber frog mold

See the Basic Technique.

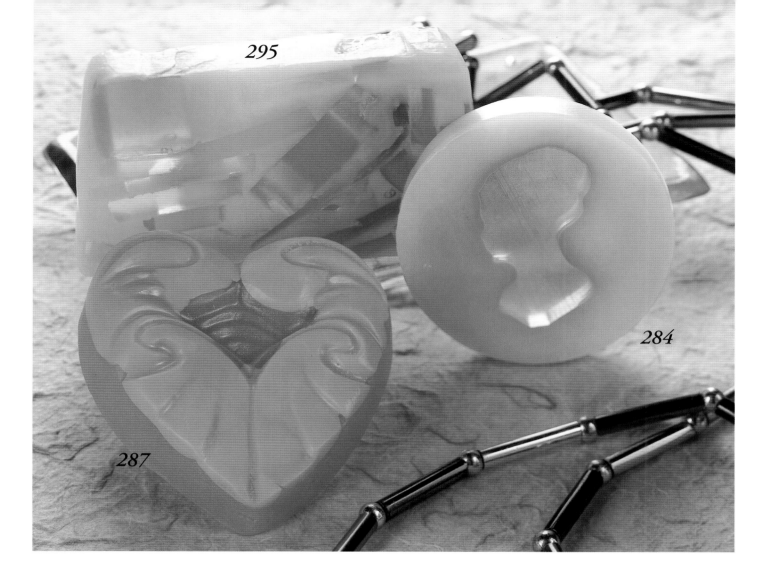

Recipe 287
Katie's Pink Heart

Katie, my 16-year-old, had to have a bar that was gentle for her skin and very pink.

Melt & Pour Base: 1-oz. pre-colored opaque pink glycerin soap base, 3 oz. fluorescent pink glycerin soap base

Fragrance: 10 drops purely pear, 10 drops vanilla

Additives: 1 teaspoon shea butter

Molds: 3.5-oz. heart with scrolls

See "Soaps with Defined Color Areas" (pour-and-scrape) in the Designer Techniques section.

Recipe 288
Harlequin

Even with simple molds you can create different effects. This mold was propped up at a 45-degree angle when the soap was poured in to create this festive layered effect. It makes two bars.

Melt & Pour Base: 2.5 oz. clear glycerin soap base, 5 oz. whitened glycerin soap base

Fragrance: 5 drops mango, 10 drops melon, 5 drops raspberry

Colorant: 3 drops luster blue (to 2.5 oz. white base), 3 drops red (to 2.5 oz. clear base), 4 drops yellow (to 2.5 oz. white base)

Molds: 4-oz. rectangle, tipped at a 45-degree angle and propped up before pouring

See "Layered Soaps" in the Designer Techniques section.

Loaf Soaps

The following loaf-style soap recipes make lots of fragrant bars of fun soap.

Recipe 289
Rainbow Loaf

Makes six large bars, 1" thick.

Melt & Pour Base: 16 oz. clear glycerin soap base

Embeds: 1/4 cup each of red, yellow, green, and blue clear soap cubes chunks

Fragrance: 20 drops raspberry, 40 drops rain

Molds: Plastic loaf mold, 4" x 6" x 3" deep

See "Chunk Style Soaps" in the Designer Techniques section.

Recipe 290
Ginger Lime Loaf

Makes six large bars, 1" thick.

Melt & Pour Base: 16 oz. clear glycerin soap base

Additives/Embeds: 1 cup clear glycerin soap base with added olive oil, cut into 1/2" cubes and six lime tube mold slices (see recipe #114)

Fragrance: 20 drops ginger, 35 drops lime

Molds: Plastic loaf mold, 4" x 6" x 3" deep

See "Chunk Style Soaps" in the Designer Techniques section.

Recipe 291
Lemonade Loaf

Makes six large bars, 1" thick.

Melt & Pour Base: 16 oz. clear glycerin soap base

Additives/Embeds: 1/2 cup clear soap cubes, 1/2 cup clear yellow soap cubes, and six lemon tube mold slices

Fragrance: 20 drops peppermint, 40 drops lemon

Molds: Plastic loaf mold, 4" x 6" x 3" deep

See "Chunk Style Soaps" in the Designer Techniques section.

Recipe 292
Lemongrass Green Tea Loaf

Makes seven large bars, 3/4" thick.

Melt & Pour Base: 24 oz. clear glycerin soap base with added hemp oil

Fragrance: 30 drops lemongrass, 30 drops green tea

Additives: 1/4 cup green tea

Molds: Plastic loaf mold, 4" x 6" x 3" deep

See the Basic Technique. Cut the slices with a garnish knife.

Recipe 293
Oatmeal 'n Honey Loaf

Makes six large bars, 1" thick.

Melt & Pour Base: 16 oz. whitened glycerin soap base with added coconut oil

Additives/Embeds: 1" x 2" soap cubes cut from clear glycerin soap base with added olive oil molded with 1/4 cup oatmeal, 20 drops honey fragrance, and 10 drops orange colorant and 4 drops blue colorant (to make an amber hue)

Fragrance: 25 drops honey almond fragrance added to white base

Molds: Plastic loaf mold, 4" x 6" x 3" deep

See "Chunk Style Soaps" in the Designer Techniques section.

Recipe 294
Lemon Poppy Loaf

Makes six large bars, 1" thick.

Melt & Pour Base: 16 oz. whitened glycerin soap base with added coconut oil

Additives/Embeds: 1" x 2" soap cubes cut from clear glycerin soap base molded with 1/4 cup poppy seeds, 30 drops lemon fragrance, and 15 drops yellow colorant

Fragrance: 25 drops sugar cookie fragrance added to white base

Molds: Plastic loaf mold, 4" x 6" x 3" deep

See "Chunk Style Soaps" in the Designer Techniques section.

289

291

290

Recipe 295
Shelter Soap

This is another great idea from soapmaker and author Kaila Westerman. When you create with melt and pour soap bases you end up with lots of soap scraps. Here's a way to use them. Kaila molds hers in a large bucket and provides instructions to the staff at shelters on how to cut the soap into bars. This makes six large bars, 1" thick.

Melt & Pour Base: 16 oz. whitened glycerin soap base

Embeds: Soap scraps, any and all colors and scents

Molds: Plastic containers, 4" x 6" x 3" deep (I like to use disposable plastic containers that come with lids and are microwave-safe. They are easy to fill, the lids keep the soap fresh, and they are easy for the shelter to use.)

See "Chunk Style Soaps" in the Designer Techniques section. Place the scraps in a loaf mold. When it's full, pour in white soap base.

Recipe 296
Pear Musk Loaf

Makes six large bars, 1" thick.

Melt & Pour Base: 10 oz. whitened glycerin soap base with added coconut oil

Embeds: 2" diameter by 6" long soap column made with 1 cup clear glycerin soap base with added hemp oil soap cubes and 8 oz. whitened glycerin soap base with 10 drops orange colorant, 4 drops blue colorant, and 30 drops pear fragrance. An additional 1/2 cup of soap cubes was placed in the mold with the soap column on top.

Fragrance: 25 drops musk fragrance, 10 drops pineapple, and 10 drops vanilla added to whitened glycerin soap base

Molds: Plastic loaf mold, 4" x 6" x 3" deep

See "Chunk Style Soaps" in the Designer Techniques section.

Message Soaps

These soaps convey messages – pictorial or verbal. They're great for commemorating a special occasion and make wonderful party favors.

297

Recipe 297
Photo Soaps

These three photo soaps show the transfer on a curved surface, a colored surface, and a clear base. Most photos show up best on a white base.

Melt & Pour Base: 6 oz. coconut oil base, 5 oz. clear glycerin soap base

Fragrance: 5 drops rose (in 2 oz. white base), 10 drops cranberry (in 4 oz. white base), 10 drops peppermint (in clear soap base)

Colorant: 2 drops red (in 2 oz. white soap base)

Molds: 4-oz. rectangle, 2-oz. heart, and 5-oz. square

Other Supplies: Family photos printed on transfer paper with a color photocopier

See "Soaps with Decals" in the Designer Techniques section.

Recipe 298
Wedding Soap

Tube soaps are a wonderful way to make lots of beautiful soap slices easily. My niece Renee designed these soaps for her wedding to Shawn. With the help of her bridesmaids, we made 130 bars as gifts for the celebration. Renee helped to choose the colors and scents and helped design the laminated label. Each tube makes 8 slices, 3/4" thick.

Melt & Pour Base: 18 oz. clear glycerin soap base

Fragrance: 20 drops lavender, 30 drops vanilla

Colorant: 20 drops yellow, 10 drops white

Molds: 3" blossom-shaped plastic tube mold

Accents: Pressed floral arrangement and lettering color photocopied and laminated

See "Tube Molded Soaps" and "Laminated Soaps" in the Designer Techniques section.

299

298

Recipe 299
Saying Soap

The idea for this soap came from my mother-in-law Betty, who deserves credit for lots of my ideas. It's an easy way to add a saying or an inspirational word embedded right into the soap. This makes one bar.

Melt & Pour Base: 4 oz. clear glycerin soap base

Fragrance: 5 drops vanilla, 5 drops mixed spice

Embeds: 2" x 3" piece of clear acetate

Molds: 4-oz. rectangle

See "Laminated Soaps" and "Embedded Soaps" in the Designer Techniques section. Write the inspirational words on clear acetate with a permanent black pen and protect with clear laminating film. Be sure to trim the corners round so there are no sharp points.

Recipe 300
The End

This is the end! It makes one bar.

Melt & Pour Base: 3 oz. clear glycerin soap base

Embeds: 2" x 3" piece of clear acetate

Molds: 3-oz. rectangle

See "Laminated Soaps" and "Embedded Soaps" in the Designer Techniques section. Write "THE END" on clear acetate with a permanent black pen and protect with clear laminating film. Trim the corners round so there are no sharp points.

Metric Conversion Chart

INCHES TO MILLIMETERS AND CENTIMETERS

Inches	MM	CM
1/8	3	.3
1/4	6	.6
3/8	10	1.0
1/2	13	1.3
5/8	16	1.6
3/4	19	1.9
7/8	22	2.2
1	25	2.5
1-1/4	32	3.2
1-1/2	38	3.8
1-3/4	44	4.4
2	51	5.1
3	76	7.6
4	102	10.2
5	127	12.7
6	152	15.2
7	178	17.8
8	203	20.3
9	229	22.9
10	254	25.4
11	279	27.9
12	305	30.5

YARDS TO METERS

Yards	Meters
1/8	.11
1/4	.23
3/8	.34
1/2	.46
5/8	.57
3/4	.69
7/8	.80
1	.91
2	1.83
3	2.74
4	3.66
5	4.57
6	5.49
7	6.40
8	7.32
9	8.23
10	9.14

Index

Index